Get Rich Organizing

The Professional Organizers Survival Guide to Launch, Manage, and Grow a Profitable Business

By
Anne M. Blumer, CPO®

Published in 2009
By SolutionsForYou, Inc.
Portland, OR 97219
www.solutionsforyou.com
www.professionalorganizertraininginstitute.com

©2009 SolutionsForYou, Inc.
ISBN 978-0-578-02051-8
Get Rich Organizing

To my husband, Stefan, and my children, Alex and Hannah, without your constant loving support, sacrifices, and encouragement, *Get Rich Organizing* would not exist. You have been my inspiration and my anchor. I am tremendously blessed and grateful you are in my life. Thank you!

Table of Contents

PART II: YOUR CLIENTELE

Acknowledgments

I would like to acknowledge two of my colleagues, Danielle Liu and Megan Spears, who have been an inspiration to me both as a professional organizer and as a businesswoman. I greatly admire, value, and appreciate their wisdom and creativity, and I am grateful for their friendship.

I want to thank all of the participants who have attended a training program with me. I have learned and improved because of your questions and suggestions.

I want to thank all of my clients who have entrusted me with their fears, personal possessions, and faith that I will guide them to a better way of living.

Introduction

Do you love to organize? Do you dream of running your own business? You can do both and earn a great salary, too! You don't have to suffer through figuring out how to start your own professional organizing business. This book is content rich and full of proven methodologies, processes, checklists, forms, systems, client case studies, and inspiration. My knowledge and experiences come from working with a broad base of clients from residential to corporate, as well as thirty years of working in corporate environments. You will benefit immediately by learning what took me years and hard lessons to know.

Getting rich is not just about making lots of money. It's about the personal fulfillment you receive from helping others learn a life skill–organizing–they so desperately need and were not taught. Watching the client have that "aha moment" when they understand what it means to "get organized" is rich beyond words.

***Get Rich Organizing* will:**
- Provide you with the knowledge and skills you need to become a successful professional organizer business owner.

- Help you cut out months or even years of annoying mistakes and learning curves, because you need to make money immediately.
- Show you how to position yourself to attract your ideal client with one hundred marketing ideas.
- Introduce you to blogging and web site development.
- Instruct you on how to clearly communicate your value and how to charge for your valuable services.
- Teach you new organizing skills and techniques to work with a variety of client types.
- Provide you with legal, insurance, and tax information to get you started in the right business entity for you and an understanding of the protection your business needs.
- Teach you proven processes and systems to organize others and transfer organizing skills.
- Tell you about real client stories that will inspire you to teach others organizing skills and keep you from making some serious mistakes in dealing with clients.
- Move you to action with recommended exercises and actions found at the end of the chapters.

Additionally you receive:
- Forms available for you to personalize with your company information saving you hours of time creating on your own.
- A listing of my top twenty-five organizing products and where to find them so you don't have to spend time researching.

- Material to create workshops on paper, time, and clutter so you can immediately market and demonstrate your organizing knowledge.
- Resources for space planning tools and web site development.
- Up-to-date industry information and trends.

The forms within this book are available for you to personalize with your company information. Any forms that are of contractual nature should be reviewed by your attorney to insure they meet with your company practices and are defensible by your attorney in the state(s) you conduct business.

I wrote *Get Rich Organizing* along with the Professional Organizer Training Institute™ curriculum, training manuals, and program because I believe in the immense value of this profession. I want others who aspire to it to represent the industry as experienced and knowledgeable professionals. I also want to share my learning in the hopes that others will benefit greatly from my experiences. I wish I had this book when I started my professional organizer business, SolutionsForYou, Inc. I would have saved time, money, and a lot of hard work. This is the book the industry has been lacking. It has everything a professional organizer needs to launch, manage, and grow a profitable business.

To deepen your knowledge of this subject and to gain hands-on client experience, consider attending one of my seminars. Program information is available at

www.professionalorganizertraininginstitute.com.

I wish you tremendous success in your career as a professional organizer business owner!

All the best,
Anne Blumer, CPO®
Professional Organizer Training Institute™
a division of SolutionsForYou, Inc.

Part I: Your Business

Chapter 1
Introduction To Professional Organizing

Description: This chapter will define the profession of organizing, provide an overview of the history of the organizing industry and of the National Association of Professional Organizers (NAPO), identify the characteristics of a professional organizer and of a business owner, explain the benefits of NAPO membership, and review the requirements for industry certification.

- Professional Organizer Definition
- How You Can Get into the Professional Organizing Business
- Characteristics of a Professional Organizer
- Characteristics of a Business Owner
- Top Ten Considerations in Becoming a Professional Organizer
- NAPO History and Overview
- Industry Trends
- NAPO Membership
- NAPO Code of Ethics
- NAPO Membership Benefits
- BCPO Certification Requirements and Preparation

PROFESSIONAL ORGANIZER DEFINITION

According to the National Association of Professional Organizers (NAPO), a professional organizer provides information, products and assistance to help others organize to *meet their needs*, guides, encourages and educates clients about basic principles of organizing by offering *support, focus and direction*, enhances the lives of clients by designing systems and processes using organizing principles and *through transferring organizing skills*, and educates the public on organizing solutions and the *resulting benefits*.

An organizer's services can range from designing an efficient closet to organizing a cross-country move. For homeowners, he or she might offer room-by-room space planning and reorganization, estate organization, improved management of paperwork and computer files, systems for managing personal finances and other records, and/or coaching in time management and goal setting.

In business settings, an organizing pro can increase productivity and profitability with improvements in paper filing and storage, electronic organizing, work-flow systems, employee time management, space design, and more.

Some professional organizers work with specific populations, such as those with attention deficit disorder (ADD), the chronically disorganized, children, seniors, or students.

From Wikipedia, the free encyclopedia, "Professional organizing is a service that helps individuals and businesses determine what to do with their items–which are generally found in a disorganized, cluttered state–then helps efficiently arrange the items and create systems to maximize the utility and visual appeal of a particular area and allow easy retrieval. A person who performs this service is a "Professional Organizer" or sometimes referred to simply as an "Organizer."

GETTING STARTED IN THE PROFESSIONAL ORGANIZING BUSINESS

There are many ways to enter the field of professional organizing. Many operate their own businesses, while others act as independent contractors or are employed by an organizing company. Those who run their own companies require business skills in addition to organizing skills. For many professional organizers, running a business is the most challenging part of the job; it is important for you to weigh this decision carefully. A small business owner wears many hats, as s(he) often serves as marketer, accountant, bookkeeper, and more.

The good news is that opportunity abounds in this industry, and you can make the choice that is comfortable for you. Should you choose to operate your own business, there are courses such as the Professional Organizer Training Institute™ geared toward helping you succeed.

Those considering a future as a professional organizer must take stock of their financial needs. Start-ups often spend 80 percent of the first year's income on marketing. Generally, the first year runs at a loss as it takes six to nine months to start generating an active client base. It is helpful to have financial resources such as credit lines and savings to draw from as you get started, and if you are currently employed, you might want to consider continuing in that job until you have an established business.

CHARACTERISTICS

This first list is of the most common characteristics a successful professional organizer demonstrates. The second list is of common characteristics a successful business owner demonstrates. Which ones do you possess? Which ones do you need to strengthen?

Professional Organizer Characteristics
- **Confident:** Always remember you know more than the client—but don't flaunt it. That will help increase your confidence, and you will appear more confident.

- **Courteous:** The ability to be gracious even when your client may not be.

- **Creative:** The ability to visualize spatially and the ability to think how to repurpose something that could become an organizing tool/container are important.

- **Credible:** Belonging to an association of your profession and obtaining education and training/certification gains you credibility.

- **Diplomatic:** You often need to be diplomatic when working with two or more clients at the same time, and sometimes you feel like a mediator.

- **Efficient:** If you are being paid by the hour, your client needs to see that you are efficient with your time/their money.

- **Empathetic:** Communicate to the client that they are not alone and that many others are in a similar state. Let them know that it's OK to ask for help.

- **Encouraging:** The ability to ask the right questions and encourage the client to come up with their own answer is important.

- **Ethical:** Maintain complete confidentiality (see NAPO's Code of Ethics later in this chapter).

- **Fun:** Organizing should be fun and not drudgery.

- **Good listener:** The ability to listen to and infer what a client means.

- **Good planner:** The ability to see the big picture and break goals down into manageable steps is needed, as is the ability to categorize and plan ahead.

- **Honest:** Your client needs to hear the truth from you.

- **Know your limitations:** Don't do anything physically outside of your limits or anything you are not trained or skilled to do.

- **Nonjudgmental:** The key to earning your client's trust is demonstrating that you are nonjudgmental of their situation.

- *Objective:* Listen to your client's view and needs with an open mind.

- *On time and prepared:* This goes hand in hand with professionalism. Walk your talk.

- *Open-minded:* Customize organizational systems to meet client needs, not yours.

- *Patient:* Being patient is very helpful when working with clients who have difficulty making decisions, have ADD, and with seniors.

- *Positive attitude:* Your client needs to hear from you that it is possible to get organized.

- *Professional:* This is how the world sees you and your business—you represent not only you, but the entire industry.

- *Respectful:* Always ask before acting. This includes taking pictures, opening drawers and cabinets, and touching anything.

Business Owner Characteristics
- *Creative:* Without the ability to think outside the box, how can you stand out from all of the other professional organizers?

- *Delegates:* Let others do what you are not best at (bookkeeping, web design, marketing, legal documents, etc.).

- *Dreamer:* See the big picture.

- *Efficient:* Be efficient with your client's time but also yours in your office.

- *Good planner:* Plan ahead with your business. What are your goals and objectives?

- *Know your limitations:* This goes hand in hand with delegating.

- *Manages time well:* Plan your day for your highest efficiency.

- *Organized:* Be prepared for working with each client, get things done on time, and be able to find what you need when you need it.

- *Problem solver:* Running a business has its risks; if you can identify what they are and have a plan to solve them, they will no longer be risks.

- *Resourceful:* Who do you need to help you do your job (handyperson, painter, interior designer, etc)? What products do you need? What are they? Where can you find them?

- **Self-disciplined:** You are your own boss now. This means you need to be disciplined to get yourself to the office every day to generate business.

- **Self-motivated:** If you can't motivate yourself, who do you know who can be your cheerleaders?

- **Self-starter:** If procrastination is an issue for you, you need to learn how to get started on areas that you are not comfortable with.

TOP TEN CONSIDERATIONS IN BECOMING A PROFESSIONAL ORGANIZER
(FROM WWW.NAPO.NET)

1. There are many ways to enter the field of professional organizing. The majority of NAPO members run their own businesses, while others act as independent contractors or are employed by an organizing company. If you choose to run your own company, you will use your organizing skills and also need to draw on business skills. The running of a business is perhaps the most important and, for some, the most daunting. There is more to running a business than being organized.

2. Be prepared to wear many hats as a small-business owner, such as accountant, marketer, bookkeeper, and the like. Don't be afraid to outsource these jobs—it pays to hire someone to do what you can't.

3. Do you prefer to work alone or with others? Many organizers thrive when working in teams. Consider collaborating with another person when you set up shop.

4. Take stock of your financial needs. Start-ups often spend 80 percent of the first year's income on marketing, with the expectation that those percentages will reverse themselves. In order to know whether this career will meet your financial goals, determine what you must make (net) in a year and work backwards from that. For example, if you need to bring home $26,000/year, you need to have $500/week coming in after all expenses and taxes are paid. That figure does not factor in vacation time, sick days, and cancellations.

5. It is helpful to have financial resources such as credit lines and savings to draw from as a start-up business. Consider obtaining a line of credit before you need it— it's easier to qualify when you don't need it than when you do.

6. These are some of the most common abilities and qualities that successful professional organizers demonstrate. Do you have what it takes?

   - Ability to listen and infer what a client means
   - Ability to customize organizational systems to meet client needs, not yours
   - Consulting/coaching skills—ability to ask the right questions to encourage the client to come up with the answer
   - Ability to teach and pass on skills
   - Ability to visualize spatially
   - Ability to see the big picture and break goals down into manageable steps
   - Ability to categorize and plan ahead

- Physical and mental endurance
- Compassion
- Responsibility
- Professionalism

7. A professional image will be important, because this is how the world sees you and your business. Credibility and professionalism go hand in hand. You'll want to put the "professional" in professional organizer. You represent not only yourself but also the entire industry.

8. Start with the area of organizing that you are passionate about, but keep an open mind to other niches to expand your horizons.

9. Expand your skills as your business develops, through reading, teleclasses, conferences, networking, and NAPO involvement.

10. Joining NAPO will keep you abreast of new products, books, and business trends in the organizing industry.

NAPO HISTORY AND OVERVIEW

The National Association of Professional Organizers (NAPO) was established in 1985 and is a nonprofit educational association whose members include organizing consultants, speakers, trainers, authors, and manufacturers of organizing products. As of this writing, NAPO has about 4,200 members across the United States and in various foreign countries. It is the largest international association of and for organizers. NAPO's mission is to develop, lead, and promote professional organizers and the organizing industry.

NATIONAL MEMBERSHIP

Join NAPO online at www.napo.net. NAPO offers two individual membership types—provisional and active. If you are a new organizer with less than one year of experience in the organizing industry, you are a *provisional* member. In addition to other NAPO benefits, provisional members receive special discounts (10 percent off of the active member conference and membership rate and 10 percent off of the active member rate for one introductory 100-level NAPO course, to be used in your provisional membership year) and a moderated e-mail discussion group dedicated solely to questions and concerns of first-year members. Provisional member dues are $180 (plus a one-time $20 processing fee).

If you have completed your provisional membership year, or are a new NAPO member with more than one year of professional organizing experience, you are an *active* member. In addition to other NAPO benefits, active members are listed in the online referral directory, participate in product development research, are entitled to voting privileges, and are eligible to hold office. Active member dues are $200 (plus a one-time $20 processing fee).

CHAPTER MEMBERSHIP

As of this writing, NAPO has thirty-five chapters. Chapter membership is voluntary, and national membership is required for chapter membership. Some chapter meetings and programs are available to nonmembers. To find a NAPO chapter in your area visit www.napo.net/who/governance/chapters.aspx.

INDUSTRY TRENDS (SOURCE: DATA WAS OBTAINED FROM VARIOUS ISSUES OF *NAPO NEWS* AND COMPILED BY AUTHOR)

The professional organizing industry has grown steadily in recent years as Americans and others all over the world attempt to gain better control of their lives. Facing more and more demands with less and less free time, consumers are struggling to manage their days and conquer the clutter and chaos building up in their lives. Increasingly, they are turning to professional organizers for help.

The following industry trends provide insight into industry growth, profession demographics, experience, wage expectations, and customer growth.

Year of Survey	1998	2003	2004	2005	2006	2007
Total Members	999	1,837	2,126	3,055	3,503	4,000
Responses	n/a	679	570	1,100	1,261	1,320
Percent of Membership (%)	n/a	38	27	36	36	33
Annual Growth (%)	n/a	17	16	44	15	14
Percent Women (%)	95	94	97	97	97	n/a
Percent Men (%)	5	6	3	3	3	n/a
Average Age	48	46	n/a	n/a	n/a	n/a
Between ages of 35 and 54 (%)	n/a	n/a	n/a	66	66	67
Bachelor's Degree (%)	43	45	48	n/a	n/a	n/a
Masters or Doctoral Degree (%)	26	26	22	n/a	n/a	n/a
Have a College Degree (%)	n/a	n/a	n/a	71	70	78
Belong to NAPO for						
Professional Credibility (%)	n/a	73	67	57	62	44
Networking (%)	n/a	27	n/a	n/a	n/a	n/a
Referral Services (%)	n/a	18	n/a	n/a	n/a	n/a
Education (%)	n/a	6	n/a	n/a	n/a	17
Other (%)	n/a	19	n/a	n/a	n/a	n/a
Member's Tenure in Professional Organizing						
0–1 Years (%)	n/a	n/a	n/a	29	n/a	n/a
2–4 Years (%)	n/a	n/a	n/a	37	n/a	n/a
5–9 Years (%)	n/a	n/a	n/a	19	n/a	n/a
10+ Years (%)	n/a	n/a	n/a	14	n/a	n/a
At least 2 years (%)						75
Business Structure						
Sole Proprietorship (%)	84	78	78	75	n/a	n/a
Partnership (%)	1	2	n/a	n/a	n/a	n/a
Corporation (%)	12	13	16	14	n/a	n/a

Year of Survey	1998	2003	2004	2005	2006	2007
LLC (%)	n/a	n/a	n/a	n/a	n/a	23
Other (%)	3	7	n/a	11	n/a	35
Top Revenue-Producing Clients						
Residential (%)	n/a	53	64	67	69	75
Home Offices (%)	n/a	19	n/a	15	14	n/a
Small Businesses (%)	n/a	17	n/a	n/a	n/a	n/a
Corporations (%)	n/a	6	n/a	n/a	n/a	n/a
Other (%)	n/a	6	n/a	n/a	n/a	n/a
Most Valuable Marketing Methods						
Referrals (%)	n/a	45	49	52	51	n/a
Networking (%)	n/a	19	n/a	19	42	n/a
Advertising (%)	n/a	9	n/a	n/a	n/a	n/a
Speaking (%)	n/a	6	n/a	n/a	n/a	n/a
Yellow Pages (%)	n/a	6	n/a	n/a	n/a	n/a
Media Coverage (%)	n/a	4	n/a	n/a	n/a	n/a
Strategic Alliances (%)	n/a	3	n/a	n/a	n/a	n/a
Other (%)	n/a	10	n/a	n/a	n/a	n/a
Other						
Average Hourly Rate	n/a	n/a	n/a	$49–$125	$49–$125	n/a
Total Clients Served by Respondents	n/a	n/a	n/a	23,600	24,597	44,730
Estimated Clients Served by All Members	n/a	n/a	n/a	70,800	86,213	135,546
Average Number of Clients Served Per Member	n/a	n/a	n/a	18	22	34

PROFESSIONAL ORGANIZER SPECIALTIES

As a professional organizer, you might specialize in one or several of the following areas of organizing specialty:

- Closet designing

- Closet organizing

- Collections/Memorabilia/Photos

- Computer consulting/Training

- Corporations

- Ergonomics

- Errands/Personal shopping

- Estate organization

- Estate sales
- Event/Meeting planning
- Filing systems
- Finances/Bookkeeping
- Garages/Attics/Basements
- Garage/Tag sales
- Health insurance claims (preparation assistance)
- Home offices
- Information management
- Kitchen organizing
- Legal offices/Medical offices
- Moving/Relocations
- Offices
- Residential seminars/Public speaking
- Space designing
- Space organizing
- Time management/Goal setting
- Wardrobe consulting
- Work with children
- Work with people who have ADD
- Work with seniors
- Work with students

NAPO CODE OF ETHICS (SOURCE: WWW.NAPO.NET)

This code of ethics is a set of principles to provide guidelines in our professional conduct with our clients, colleagues, and community.

As a member of the National Association of Professional Organizers, I pledge to exercise judgment, self-restraint, and conscience in my conduct in order to establish and maintain public confidence in the integrity of NAPO members and to preserve and encourage fair and equitable practices among all who are engaged in the profession of organizing.

Clients-Working Relationships

I will serve my clients with integrity, competence, and objectivity, and will treat them with respect and courtesy. I will offer services in those areas in which I am qualified and will accurately represent those qualifications in both verbal and written communications.

When unable or unqualified to fulfill requests for services, I will make every effort to recommend the services of other qualified organizers and/or other qualified professionals. I will advertise my services in an honest manner and will represent the organizing profession accurately.

Confidentiality

I will keep confidential all client information, both business and personal, including that which may be revealed by other organizers. I will use proprietary client information only with the client's permission. I will keep client information confidential and not use it to benefit myself or my firm, or reveal this information to others. I will not bring discredit to the organizing profession.

Fees

I will decide independently and communicate to my client in advance my fees and expenses, and will charge fees and expenses which I deem reasonable, legitimate, and commensurate with my experience, the services I deliver, and the responsibility I accept. I will make recommendations for products and services with my client's best interests in mind.

Colleagues

I will seek and maintain an equitable, honorable, and cooperative association with other NAPO members and will treat them with respect and courtesy. I will respect the intellectual property rights (materials, titles, and thematic creations) of my colleagues, and other firms and individuals, and will not use proprietary information or methodologies without permission. I will act and speak on a high professional level so as to not bring discredit to the organizing profession.

BENEFITS OF NAPO

NAPO members profit from education, networking, and professional resources. The association is always looking for more ways to enhance membership.

NAPO members enjoy exclusive access to ...

Member Benefit	National (Source: www.NAPO.net)	Chapter
Affinity programs	NAPO leverages the power of numbers so that even sole proprietors can have access to business essentials such as long-term-care insurance,	

Member Benefit	National (Source: www.NAPO.net)	Chapter
	liability insurance, prescription-drug discount card, credit-card processing, online shopping cart services, a Web site builder, and learning management system solutions.	
Conference Media		Many chapters possess media materials from several of the NAPO conferences for you to access. You have the ability to experience the conference and learn from the experienced organizers that have presented in the past.
Client Referrals	A listing in NAPO's online Professional Organizer Directory, a great way to build a client base. (For Active Members only; Provisional Members are not listed in this directory.)	Some chapters offer a structured, client referral service similar to the national one. This opportunity is only extended to chapter members.
Continuing Education	The annual NAPO conference is an opportunity for quality educational programs, networking with colleagues and exhibitors, and learning new ideas about the profession and how to better assist clients. Held each year in the spring, the conference draws professional	Offers various monthly, quarterly, and/or annual meetings that include educational opportunities.

Member Benefit	National (Source: www.NAPO.net)	Chapter
	organizers from around the globe. In addition to top-notch keynotes, the pre-conference and concurrent sessions are geared toward beginning, intermediate and advanced organizers. Exhibitors, featuring the latest organizing and time management products and services, are another conference highlight.	
Credibility with Clients	Being associated with an organization of like professionals gives an impression to clients that you are credible.	Membership and leadership in your professional association demonstrates to prospective clients that you care about your profession and are willing to participate in its development. Being a member of a local chapter reinforces this.
Golden Circle Membership	A prestigious designation available to NAPO members who have worked as a professional organizer for 5 or more years and have been a NAPO member for at least one year.	
Leadership	Leadership opportunities that provide experience, exposure, and the ability to affect the future of the organizing	Local chapters offer active NAPO members a chance to be involved as an officer, director, or committee

Member Benefit	National (Source: www.NAPO.net)	Chapter
	industry on the national and local levels (Active Members only).	chair. Share and develop your leadership skills as you shape and lead our industry. This adds credibility to yourself and positions you for PR exposure.
Membership Directory	Members-Only section of NAPO's Web site, which includes NAPO's membership directory, document library, listservs (including a moderated listserv for first-year members), access to product information and discounts, and more.	Directories are a quick and easy way to find personal and professional support. Perhaps you have a client referral or need an extra boost of confidence. Turn to your colleagues for mutual support by using a local NAPO chapter directory.
Members-only Discounts	NAPO's Annual Conference and Organizing Exposition, the Certified Professional Organizer® (CPO) program, and educational courses that include teleclasses and classroom instruction. (Provisional Members receive an additional 10 percent discount on membership, conference registration, and one introductory NAPO course.)	
Networking Opportunities	Belonging to an association of professional organizers gives you an opportunity to network and learn from	For the professional organizer working out of home or in a small office, networking is critical to

Member Benefit	National (Source: www.NAPO.net)	Chapter
	others in your profession.	staying on top of your game and counters the issues of isolation. Getting to know other qualified colleagues in your geographical area can help you with receiving or giving client referrals, provide you with professional resources, and strengthen personal and professional support.
Newsletters	NAPO News, a 20-page bimonthly newsletter filled with industry and association news, features and advice. NAPO e-News Blasts, monthly emailed newsletters featuring the latest in news and tips.	Many chapters provide members with a newsletter featuring local chapter information and member news.
Personal and Professional Support		Ever get stumped by an organizing problem or client? Ever feel that you just don't have the energy to accomplish your own business goals? The one-on-one interaction that chapter activities provide creates opportunities to become acquainted and develop close friendships with professional colleagues who understand your profession.

Member Benefit	National (Source: www.NAPO.net)	Chapter
		Remember that we're in this together!
Publicity	Public-relations and cooperative marketing efforts that build nationwide awareness of the organizing industry in both residential and business spheres.	Chapters participate in many activities that generate local media interest. The savvy professional organizers join forces with chapters and take advantage of those opportunities to generate exposure for the industry and business opportunities for themselves.
Vendor Discounts	The Industry Exchange, an online connection to NAPO's Associate Members and Industry Partners. These affiliated companies often offer their new organizing solutions and products with discounts, promotions and specials available only to NAPO members.	There may be local vendor discounts on products and services. Check with your chapter leadership for details.
Web Site Participation	The NAPO National Web site gives you visibility to clients and media.	Local chapters that have Web sites often offer members the ability to advertise at a nominal cost. Web site directories and information to the public are invaluable to the growth of your business.

CERTIFICATION

The professional organizing industry has a certification program that was developed by NAPO and is operated under the auspices of the Board of Certification for Professional Organizers® (BCPO®). The Certified Professional Organizer (CPO®) designation is a voluntary, industry-led effort that benefits the public and members of the organizing profession. CPO Certification recognizes those professionals who have met specific minimum qualifications and have proven through examination and client interaction that they possess the body of knowledge and experience required for certification. The program recognizes and raises industry standards, practices, and ethics. While the CPO designation is not an endorsement or recommendation, certification of professional organizers maximizes the value received from the services provided and products recommended by a CPO.

For more information, visit the BCPO Web site at www.certifiedprofessionalorganizers.org or call the BCPO headquarters at 800.556.0484.

CERTIFICATION REQUIREMENTS OF THE BOARD OF CERTIFIED PROFESSIONAL ORGANIZERS (SOURCE: WWW.CERTIFIEDPROFESSIONALORGANIZERS.ORG):

1. Qualified candidates must have a minimum of a high school diploma.

2. As a part of the application process, candidates must agree to adhere to the code of ethics.

3. www.certifiedprofessionalorganizers.org/COE.html.

4. Candidates must be prepared to document a total of

1,500 hours of *paid* work experience in the last three years. Paid work experience may include on-site organizing, coaching, consulting, training, virtual organizing, interactive workshops and speaking engagements, or any form of paid work experience, which, through client interaction, transfers or teaches organizing skills.

Up to 250 substitute hours of the required 1,500 can be earned via college degrees, continuing education courses, or professional development activities in the organizing field. Substitute hours may also be earned via organizing related writing and speaking, or relevant paid work experience prior to becoming an organizer and accrued in the three years prior to the application date, as detailed below.

Candidates may claim a maximum of 250 hours of credit toward the required 1,500 hours of paid work experience from one or more of the following substitute categories:

Formal Education (noncumulative, 100 hours credit maximum)
- AA Degree, fifty hours credit
- Bachelor Degree, seventy-five hours credit
- Advanced Degree, one hundred hours credit

Organizing-Related Professional Activities
(within the last three years)
- Paid speaking engagements, actual hours, maximum of ten hours credit

- Mentor/mentee/apprenticeship, actual hours, maximum of ten hours credit

- Publishing books, twenty per book, maximum of forty hours credit

- Authoring articles (minimum 500 words per article), ten per article, maximum of thirty hours credit

- Professional association membership, maximum of ten hours credit

- Trainer/teacher, maximum of ten hours credit

- Serving on an organizing entity's board of directors, maximum of ten hours credit

- Volunteer work as an organizer, maximum of ten hours credit

Continuing Education Courses Relating to Organizing (within the last three years)

For each course, the candidate may claim the actual hours attended, to a cumulative total of 250 hours. Sixty minutes of coursework is equal to one credit hour regardless of any number of continuing education credits (CEUs) another institution may have awarded for completion of the course.

Relevant Paid Work Experience Prior to Becoming an Organizer

Twenty-five per full-time year (maximum three years or seventy-five hours credit.) Experience must include the same criteria for transfer of skills as described in the 1,500 hours requirement.

Cost

Currently the cost is $375 for NAPO or Professional Organizers in Canada (POC) members and $550 for nonmembers.

Application

You can find the application online at the BCPO website location: www.certifiedprofessionalorganizers.org/BCPO_CPO_Applicat ion_Form.pdf.

Recertification

After initial certification, recertification is required every three years to ensure that a practitioner maintains his or her competence over time. The certificant must recertify prior to the expiration of the current three-year certification period, or he or she will be treated as a new candidate. Recertification may be achieved by either (a) asserting one thousand hours of paid work in any area related to organizing, plus earning forty-five organizing-related continuing education hours, during the three-year period, or (b) retaking the examination. If the individual chooses to recertify by examination and fails, he or she may not then recertify via the experience/continuing education method, and the prior certification is immediately revoked. Providing the eligibility requirements are met, he or she would be eligible to submit a new application for future examinations.

BCPO Certification Examination Recommended Reading List (subject to change):

Author	Title
BCPO	Code of Ethics for Certified Professional Organizers
Allen, David	*Getting Things Done*
Baker, Sunny	*The Complete Idiot's Guide to Project Management*
Bruce, Andy, and Ken Langdon	*Essential Managers: Project Management*
Goldberg, Donna	*The Organized Student*
Jasmine, Grace	*Fabjob Guide to Become a Professional Organizer*
Knight, Porter	*Organized to Last*
Kolberg, Judith	*Conquering Chronic Disorganization*
Lehmkuhl, Dorothy, and Lamping, Dolores Cotter	*Organizing for the Creative Person*
Mark, Teri	*Organize Your Office: A Small Business Survival Guide to Managing Records*
McCorry, K. J.	*Organize Your Work Day in No Time*
Morgenstern, Julie	*Organizing from the Inside Out*
Morgenstern, Julie	*Time Management from the Inside Out*
Roth, Eileen, and Elizabeth Miles	*Organizing for Dummies*
Seidler, Cindi	*A Manual for Professional Organizers*

Author	Title
Silver, Susan	*Organized to Be Your Best!*
Smallin, Donna	*Organizing Plain and Simple*
Stanley, Debbie	*Ethical Pitfalls*
Taylor, Harold	*Making Time Work for You* (old and new editions)
Tiani, Jackie	*Organizing for a Living*
Waddill, Kathy	*The Organizing Sourcebook: Nine Strategies for Simplifying Your Life*
Walsh, Peter	*It's All Too Much*
Winston, Stephanie	*Getting Organized* (2006 edition)

OTHER INDUSTRY ASSOCIATIONS

- National Study Group on Chronic Disorganization (NSGCD) www.nsgcd.org

- Professional Organizers in Canada (POC) www.organizersincanada.com

- National Association of Senior Move Managers (NASMM) www.nasmm.org

✍ EXERCISES

➤ From the list of characteristics, which ones could you improve upon?

➤ What area(s) will you specialize in?

📄 ACTIONS

☐ Join NAPO.

☐ Research liability insurance.

☐ Set up a tracking system for certification hours and supporting documentation.

☐ Read from the BCPO recommended reading list, even if you are not planning to certify at this time.

Chapter 2

Assessing Your Skills

Description: This chapter will review your skills, prior experience, and education as it relates to the field of professional organizer, will discuss why you want to be one.

- How can your background and education work for you?

- Why do you want to be a professional organizer?

- What professional organizer characteristics do you possess?

- What business owner characteristics do you possess?

- What is a typical day like for a professional organizer?

- What is a typical day like for a business owner?

Most professional organizers who do not succeed do so not because they can't organize but because they don't know how to start and run a business. Understanding your strengths, background, experience, and characteristics will help you to succeed not only as a professional organizer but as a professional organizer business owner.

WHAT ARE YOUR STRENGTHS?

- What characteristics from Chapter 1 do you possess?

- Do you meet people easily the first time? If not, why? You might want to work on referrals from people you know only.

- What people skills do you possess (courteous, friendly, good listener, diplomatic, empathetic, encouraging, honest, nonjudgmental, patient, respectful)?

- Are you comfortable speaking in front of a group? Public speaking is a great marketing venue if you do.

- Have you managed projects before? What were they? What project management skills do you possess (manage time well, ability to break down into tasks, delegate, efficient, problem solver, resourceful)?

- Have you always been an organized person or have you learned how to be one? If you have not always been an organized person, you will be able to relate better to your clients than professional organizers who have always been organized.

WHAT IS YOUR BACKGROUND?

- Where have you lived?

- Have you moved often?

- Married, single, divorced, have children?

- Did you attend/graduate from college?

These are life transitions, and life transitions are a key factor in why and when organization systems break down for your clients.

WHAT IS YOUR JOB EXPERIENCE?

- Have you always worked outside the home or never?

- Have you been a stay-at-home parent or a working parent?

- Have you worked in corporate and did you like it? If you have not worked in corporate, you may not be comfortable working with corporate clients.

- Have you worked in small businesses or have you owned your own business?

- Do you like being the boss?

- Do you work well with others or prefer to work alone?

A TYPICAL DAY FOR A PROFESSIONAL ORGANIZER

A typical day working with clients might include any one or more of the following activities:

- Cleaning out closets, kitchens, storage areas, bedrooms, attics, and garages, etc. In other words, basic decluttering

- Remodeling closets and storage spaces

- Rearranging living space to be more pleasing and efficient

- Personal coaching and goal setting

- Planning, packing, and unpacking for relocation

- Garage and estate sales

- Organizing children and teenagers

- Errands and personal shopping

- Computer organizing and training

- Setting up filing systems and developing paper-flow systems

- Information management systems

- Accounting and bookkeeping

- Filing

- Setting up record-keeping systems

- Sorting through paper piles

- Paying bills

- Developing procedures manuals

- Preparing medical insurance forms

- Event planning

- Disaster preparedness

- Photo and memorabilia organization

- Time management training

- Seminars and public speaking

In addition, organizers may work with:

- People in their homes

- Small businesses

- Large businesses

- Clients with attention deficit disorder

- People with chronic disorganization problems

- Students

- Seniors

- Individuals

- Groups

Obviously all professional organizers don't do all of these things! Most will specialize in one or more areas.

A TYPICAL DAY FOR A BUSINESS OWNER

Business owners will typically need to address one or more of the following areas on any given day:

- Invoicing clients

- Recording expenses and income

- Balancing your checking account

- Reviewing your financials

- Writing marketing materials

- Writing a newsletter

- Preparing for tax filing or meeting with your tax accountant

- Running payroll (even if you are a one person organization)

- Interviewing and hiring employees or subcontractors

- Scheduling employees or subcontractors

- Developing your Web site

- Reviewing and updating your business plan and goals

Your background, experience, skills, characteristics, and business goals will determine what your typical day will be like as a professional organizer business owner and determine where you need to gain skills and resources to be successful as both.

✍ EXERCISES

✦ What does all of this say about you? Take a few minutes and write on a piece of paper what you have done in your life that will make you a good professional organizer. What your unique abilities?

✦ What do you like to do from the list of typical activities for a professional organizer and a business owner?

✦ What don't you like to do from the list of typical activities for a professional organizer and a business owner?

Chapter 3

Writing a Business Plan

Description: Your business plan is often an afterthought if it is ever addressed at all. In this chapter you will learn the value of writing a business plan and how it can save you from costly mistakes.

- Define your business concept.

- Develop your mission statement.

- Determine who your key client is and how you will attract them.

- Describe what services and products you will offer.

- Research your competition.

- Define your goals and objectives.

- Develop your financial plan.

- Detail your action plan.

- Identify your resource requirements.

- Perform a S.W.O.T analysis.

The real value of creating a business plan is not in having the finished written plan in hand. Rather, the value lies in the process of researching and thinking about your business in a systematic way. The act of planning helps you think things through thoroughly, study and research if you are not sure of the facts, and look at your ideas critically. It takes time now, but avoids costly, perhaps disastrous, mistakes later.

I didn't write a business plan the first two years I was in business, and I didn't experience any growth in my business either. Since writing my business plan and updating it each year, my business has experienced significant growth each and every year.

It typically takes several weeks to complete a good plan. Most of that time is spent in research and rethinking your ideas and assumptions. But then, that's the value of the process. So make time to do the job properly. Those who do, never regret the effort. And finally, be sure to keep detailed notes on your sources of information and on the assumptions underlying your financial data and review with your attorney and accountant.

QUESTIONS TO ASK BEFORE WRITING YOUR BUSINESS PLAN

- Is this a hobby, a job, a business, or are you an entrepreneur?

- What does it take to manage each of these entities?

- What are the time commitments for each of these, whether you are a doer, manager, president, or all three? How can you schedule time for each of these roles?

BUSINESS CONCEPT

- Summarize the key technology, concept, or strategy on which your business is based. This can be as basic as people need help organizing their paper, time, and space, or, people need to learn organizing skills.

MISSION STATEMENT

Your mission statement is a clear statement of your company's long-term mission. Many companies have a brief mission statement, usually in fifty words or less, explaining their reason for being and their guiding principles.

Example:

To provide confidential and empathetic advice to our clients, identify their individual organizing challenges, and attain and maintain organization by working with them to create solutions and sustainable systems that will increase their productivity, reduce stress, and lead to more control over their surroundings.

It says *what you will do for the client* (provide confidential and empathetic advice to our clients, identify their individual organizing challenges, and attain and maintain organization) and *how* (by working with them to create solutions and sustainable systems) and *the benefits* of working with you (will increase their productivity, reduce stress, and lead to more control over their surroundings).

MARKET AND CUSTOMER ANALYSIS

Review those changes in market share, leadership, players, market shifts, costs, pricing, or competition that provide the opportunity for your company's success. Identify your key clients, their characteristics, and their geographic locations, otherwise known as their demographics. You may have more than one client group (residential, home-based business, small business, corporate). Identify the most important groups. Then, for each client group, construct what is called a demographic profile.

For residential customers the demographic factors might be:

- Age

- Gender

- Location

- Income level

- Social class and occupation

- Education

- Learning disability

For business customers, the demographic factors might be:

- Industry (or portion of an industry)

- Location

- Size of firm

- Quality, technology, and price preferences

STRATEGY

Outline a marketing strategy that is consistent with your niche. Will you have important indirect competitors? For example, video rental stores compete with theaters, although they are different types of businesses. How will your products or services compare with the competition? See Chapter 9 for more information on marketing strategies.

OPPORTUNITIES (PROBLEMS AND OPPORTUNITIES)

State your client's problems, and define the nature of product and service opportunities that are created by those problems. What are the needs and how can you fill them? What are some problems and symptoms that your clients have? What do they want from you? What is so important that they are willing to pay you to provide solutions for them? These are people you need to be marketing to. You don't have to work with everyone!

Example

A common consumer problem is clients have tried to set up a file system, but they never use it.

The opportunity for you is to offer your clients a universal prepackaged filing system that (a) solves the client's problem and (b) can provide you with product revenue because you can buy the filing systems in quantity and receive a wholesale price from the vendor and keep the mark-up for you.

PRODUCTS AND SERVICES

Describe your products and services as you see them and, more importantly, how your client sees them. What factors will give you competitive advantages or disadvantages? Examples may include level of quality or unique or proprietary features. What are the fees of your products or services? Describe the most important features. What is special about your services? Describe the benefits. That is, what will your services do for the client? What after-sale services will you give? Some examples are guarantee, support, follow-up, and refund policy.

COMPETITION

Summarize your competition. What are they doing? How can you do it better? Outline your company's competitive advantage. List your major competitors. Will they compete with you across the board, or just for certain products, certain clients, or in certain locations? Will you have important indirect competitors? How will your products or services compare with the competition?

NICHE

Now that you have systematically analyzed your industry, your clients, and the competition, you should have a clear picture of where your company fits into the world. In one short paragraph, define your niche, your unique corner of the market.

GOALS AND OBJECTIVES

Goals are destinations. Where do you want your business to be? Objectives are progress markers along the way to achieving your goals. For example, a goal might be to move from working part-time to full-time after two years. An objective of that goal might be to increase client billable time from ten hours a week to twenty hours a week.

FINANCIAL PLAN

The financial plan consists of your start-up costs, a twelve month profit and loss projection, a cash-flow projection, a projected balance sheet, and a break-even calculation. Together they constitute a reasonable estimate of your company's financial future. More important, the process of thinking through the financial plan will improve your insight into the inner financial workings of your company. QuickBooks and Quicken for Small Businesses are excellent software programs for tracking revenue and expenses and for producing business and tax reports.

The following table includes expenses professional organizers should consider in their business financial planning.

EXPENSES	Amount
Formation and Licensing:	
Business license	$
Business registration	$
Legal advice	$
Tax advice	$
Trademark	$
Web Presence:	
Domain	$
Web design	$
Web hosting	$
Business Materials:	
Brochures, info packet	$
Business cards	$
Advertising:	
Online Ad, Community Newspaper Ad, Yellow pages, etc.	$
Marketing:	
Logo/Branding design (should be one-time expense)	$
Office Equipment:	
Computer, phone, printer, copier, fax, etc. (see Chapter 5)	$
Field Equipment:	
Camera, label maker, step stool, drill, etc. (see Chapter 5)	$
Office Supplies:	$
Professional Development:	
NAPO membership, NAPO conference, other industry memberships and conferences	$
Professional Services:	
Tax preparation	$
Insurance:	$
Taxes:	$
Office Space:	$
TOTAL Expenses (breakeven point)	$
Projected Receivables	$
PROFIT or LOSS (Receivables minus Expenses)	$

GETTING STARTED

Your project plan or actions list is everything you need to do to launch your business including (in the order they should be completed):

1. Professional development

2. Business plan

3. Budget

4. Domain registration—Research availability and cost (www.whois.net)

5. Business name

6. Meet with accountant

7. Meet with attorney

8. Business registry

9. Obtain Federal tax ID number (www.irs.gov/pub/irs-pdf/fss4.pdf)

10. Business license

11. E-mail account

12. Checking account

13. Set up Quicken, Quickbooks, or other financial record keeping system

14. Set up time-management system to track client sessions.

15. Find a client!

16. Identify external resources (handyperson, painter, interior designer, etc).

17. Logo and tagline (www.elogocontest.com and www.thelogocompany.net are online examples)

18. Web site design

19. Register trademark (www.uspto.gov)

20. Professional pictures

21. Media kit materials

RESOURCE REQUIREMENTS

Technology resource requirements include items such as a computer, phone, printer, copier, and fax. Personnel requirements include employees, associates, independent contractors. Professional requirements include CPA, attorney, marketing, and webmaster. External requirements are products or services for your clients that must be purchased outside the company.

KEY ISSUES

Isolate key decisions and issues that need immediate or near-term resolution. Also isolate issues needing long-term resolution. State the consequences of decision postponement. If you are seeking funding, state specifics of both near and long-term key issues.

RISKS (THREATS) AND REWARDS

Summarize the risks of the business and how the risks will be addressed. What rewards do you hope to receive? They can be monetary, personal fulfillment, or both.

S.W.O.T. ANALYSIS

This is a powerful technique for identifying *strengths* and *weaknesses*, and for examining the *opportunities* and *threats* you face. Used in a personal context, it helps you develop your career in a way that takes best advantage of your talents, abilities, and opportunities.

What makes S.W.O.T. particularly powerful is that with a little thought, it can help you uncover opportunities that you are well placed to take advantage of. By understanding your weaknesses, you can manage and eliminate threats that would otherwise catch you unawares.

How to Use the Tool

To complete a S.W.O.T. analysis, use the S.W.O.T. matrix below, and write down answers to the following questions:

Strengths:	Weaknesses:
• What do you do well? • What unique resources can you draw on? • What do others see as your strengths? • What advantages (for example, skills, education, or connections) do you have that others don't have? • What do you do better than anyone else?	• What could you improve? • What resources are you lacking? • What should you avoid (due to lack of skills, training, physical limitations, etc.)? • What are others likely to see as your weaknesses?

• What personal resources do you have access to?	
Opportunities: • What good opportunities are open to you? • What trends could you take advantage of? • How can you turn your strengths into opportunities? • What are the interesting trends you are aware of?	**Threats:** • What trends could hurt you? • What is your competition doing? • What threats do your weaknesses expose you to?

Strengths

Consider this from your own perspective, and from the point of view of the people around you. Don't be modest. Be as objective as you can. If you are having any difficulty with this, try writing down a list of your characteristics (see Chapter 1).

In looking at your strengths, think about them in relation to the people around you. For example, if you're a great organizer and the people around you are great at organizing, then this is not likely to be a strength in your current role; it is likely to be a necessity or even a threat.

Weaknesses

Again, consider this from a personal and external basis: Do other people perceive weaknesses that you do not see? Do co-workers consistently out-perform you in key areas? It is best to be realistic now, and face any unpleasant truths as soon as possible.

Opportunities

Useful opportunities can come from such things as changes in technology, markets, your company on both a broad and narrow scale, changes in certification related to your field, changes in social patterns, population profiles, lifestyle changes, etc., or local events.

A useful approach to looking at opportunities is also to look at your strengths and ask yourself whether these open up any opportunities. Alternatively, look at your weaknesses and ask yourself whether you could open up opportunities by eliminating them.

Threats

What obstacles do you face? What are the people around you doing? Is your job (or the demand for the things you do) changing? Is changing technology threatening your position? Could any of your weaknesses seriously threaten you?

A S.W.O.T. matrix is a framework for analyzing your internal strengths and weaknesses, and the external opportunities and threats you face. This helps you to focus on your strengths, minimize weaknesses, and take the greatest possible advantage of opportunities available. Carrying out this analysis will often be illuminating—both in terms of pointing out what needs to be done, and in putting problems into perspective.

📄 **ACTIONS**

☐ Complete your business plan.

☐ Perform your S.W.O.T. analysis.

☐ Start your action list—set goals for completing each task.

Chapter 4

Fee Structures

How to Charge for Your Services

Description: Establishing your fee continues to be the one area where many professional organizers undervalue their services. This chapter covers how to determine a reasonable market rate, earn the income you desire, and communicate your value to clients.

- Selling your value

- Describe the benefits (value) your client will receive

- Hourly fee vs. project fee

- Initial consultation—fee or free?

- Travel fee

- Materials fee

- National average

- How to determine a reasonable market fee

- When and how to give yourself a raise

SELLING YOUR VALUE

The client needs to understand the value of your services. It's hard for a client to know whether your fee is affordable or reasonable until they have had a chance to understand the value of your services to them. If you charge a dollar an hour but don't produce anything of value, your services are too expensive. If you charge $500 an hour and transform someone's life, they need you, and they need to figure out how they can hire you. A person who sees and understands the value of something and wants it can always figure out a way to make it happen if you can make a case for the value of what you do, and thus you can ask a higher fee.

HOW TO DESCRIBE THE BENEFITS (VALUE) YOUR CLIENT WILL RECEIVE

Feature benefits include:
- You have a proven organizing process.

- You will set up systems that will work.

- You will help your client to pick the right containers.

Functional benefits provide your client with:
- More time

- Ability to find things

- Financial savings

- More space

Emotional benefits provide your client with:

- Peace of mind

- Less stress

- Control

- Confidence

- A sense of calm

Inspirational benefits provide your client with:

- The ability to achieve their goals

- A sense of freedom

- Clarity, hope, and possibility

- A sense of empowerment

- Increased focus and productivity

HOURLY FEE VERSUS PROJECT FEE

Most organizers charge by the hour. Some organizers offer sliding scale rates if a client wants to purchase blocks of hours, similar to a personal trainer. Think carefully about what your time is worth and be careful not to low-ball or undercharge your fee just to get the job. If you believe in your worth, your client will, too. There may be occasions to charge on a project fee basis—whole house organizing or corporate projects. For projects you might want to add 15 to 20 percent above your fee to account for additional outside time doing research or shopping and to cover additional time of what you originally estimate.

INITIAL CONSULTATION AND NEEDS ASSESSMENT

Many organizers do not charge for the initial consultation and needs assessment (usually no more than one hour). Others don't charge for a follow-up consultation. I do a pretty thorough complimentary assessment on my Web site (including uploading pictures of their organizing project) and over the phone when a prospect contacts me. This time spent is for my benefit because I'm assessing the problem areas and gathering information about the person's organizing project and other data to determine if I like them and if we'd be a good fit for each other. I'm fact-finding and this assessment is for my benefit. I'm the one learning, and I'm not giving them information or solutions, so why would they pay for that?

On the other hand, the consultation is something I do charge for, and it happens after we've had a phone conversation. I go into the space, already knowing fairly well what I'm walking into because I've spent some time on the phone with the client in advance and they have sent me photographs. The session typically lasts one to two hours. I come in and do a thorough tour of the space, ask a lot of questions, offer verbal suggestions, and in the end, I send them (via e-mail) a comprehensive written Organizing Plan of Action from which to work. They can then choose to implement it themselves or hire me to work with them. The client pays for the consultation because they are learning exactly what they need to do to remedy their situation. If you clarify who is receiving the information and the benefit, then you'll know whether you're doing an assessment or a consultation.

TRAVEL FEE

You might consider charging a travel fee for clients who ask you to come to their home/office that is over X miles or over X time.

MATERIALS FEE

Materials are exclusive of your hourly fee and are reimbursable expenses. Some vendors offer NAPO members discounts. You may want to pass this discount on to your client, or you may want to keep the discount and not charge your client the time you spend purchasing the materials. Or, you may want to charge a materials procurement (shopping) fee.

NATIONAL AVERAGE

The best way to determine a fee to charge your clients is to understand what professional organizers in your area are charging for similar services. Do *not* call professional organizers in your area pretending to be a potential client to find out their fee. You can research other professional organizers Web sites; many list their fee on their services page. You might research other similar professional services fees such as a personal trainer, personal chef, and personal or business coach.

ARTICLES QUOTING PROFESSIONAL ORGANIZER FEES

- *Newsweek* article "Clean Freaks," 2004: $50–$200/hr.

- *New York Times* article "A Clutter Too Deep for Mere Bins and Shelves," January 1, 2008: $60–$100/hr.

- *NAPO News* June-July 2005 "Who Are We? Highlights of the 2005 NAPO Membership Survey," $49 to more than $125/hr.

How to Determine a Reasonable Market Fee

When deciding what to charge, use this simple formula. Take an arbitrary net annual salary figure (such as $36,000).

Add the cost of benefits such as vacation, sick days, health and disability insurance, life insurance, and retirement plans.

Add in expenses such as utilities, supplies, equipment, and office rent. This equals the gross annual salary needed.

Next, divide this total by the number of hours you can *realistically* expect to work in a year. Due to holidays, vacation, sick days, professional development, and office time, the typical full-time professional *realistically* bills about fifteen out of twenty working days a month, or 720 hours a year (15 days x 12 months x 4 hours a day).

The result will be the amount you should charge per hour.

It is important to note that you will put in many non-billable hours doing your own administrative and marketing work.

Example

Disclaimer: This is only an example of how the formula calculates and is not a service rate recommendation. This worksheet is not intended to suggest any minimum or maximum rates.

Desired [net] Annual Salary	$36,000.00	$36,000.00
+Benefits and Expenses (50 percent)	50%	$18,000.00
Total [gross] Annual Salary		$54,000.00
Divided by Hours Worked 720 = Hourly Rate to Charge	720	**$75.00**

WHEN AND HOW TO GIVE YOURSELF A RAISE

Eventually, you'll probably be able to raise your fee as you gain more experience. When you do raise your fee, raise it for past clients as well. For clients you are currently working on a project with you could charge your new fee for future projects with them.

FINAL WORD ON FEES

The client wants choices. Without having a different fee for different services, you need to find a way to provide your client choices. For example: Hourly fee with the option of (1) hands-on organizing (will cost more), or (2) a plan (probably the least expensive), or (3) a combination of the two. This gives the client three cost choices without different fees.

☐ ACTIONS

☐ What fee will you charge?

☐ Will you charge by the hour or by the project?

☐ How will you structure your fees?

Chapter 5

Business Basics

OFFICE BASICS CHECKLIST

Office Space

Office Equipment and Furniture
- ✓ Book shelves
- ✓ Comfortable chair
- ✓ Computer
- ✓ Copier (optional)
- ✓ Data backup
- ✓ Desk
- ✓ Filing cabinet
- ✓ Phone
- ✓ Printer (preferably color)
- ✓ Scanner (optional)
- ✓ Shredder

Software
- ✓ Accounting and bookkeeping (such as Quickbooks)
- ✓ Contact management (such as Microsoft Outlook)
- ✓ Internet browser, E-mail, Virus protection, Firewall
- ✓ Productivity suite (Microsoft Office, Open Office, Apple iWork, etc.)

Record Keeping
- ✓ Client files
- ✓ Deposits and paid invoices
- ✓ Expense receipts
- ✓ Quicken for tracking expenses/income
- ✓ Tax records
- ✓ Time management system, either paper or electronic

Business Forms
- ✓ Assessment questionnaire
- ✓ Client appraisal form
- ✓ Client intake form (initial client contact checklist)
- ✓ Invoices
- ✓ Letter of agreement
- ✓ Phone log
- ✓ Proposals (organizing plan of action)

Filing System specific to your business

Supplies
- ✓ 3-hole punch
- ✓ Binders w/dividers
- ✓ Calculator
- ✓ Hanging folders
- ✓ Label maker
- ✓ Manila folders

Information Supplies
- ✓ Business cards
- ✓ Catalogs of organizing products

- ✓ Client references
- ✓ Letterhead, envelopes
- ✓ Listing of your services in a flyer or brochure
- ✓ Portfolio
- ✓ Presentations
- ✓ Resource list (products, Web sites, donation services, handyperson, etc.)
- ✓ Thank-you cards

FIELD MATERIALS CHECKLIST

Field Materials
- ✓ Client file
    - ✓ Intake Form (Initial Client Contact Checklist)
    - ✓ Agreement
    - ✓ Invoice
    - ✓ Proposal (Needs Assessment and Plan of Action)
    - ✓ Directions/Map
- ✓ Business Cards
- ✓ Camera
- ✓ Flash light
- ✓ First-aid kit
- ✓ Information packet/Tip sheets
- ✓ Mileage book
- ✓ Stepladder

Tool Kit
- ✓ Air filter mask
- ✓ Disinfectant wipes
- ✓ Band-aids
- ✓ Eraser

- ✓ Furniture moving discs
- ✓ Hammer
- ✓ Label maker, extra label tape, batteries
- ✓ Marking pens
- ✓ Paper clips and binder clips
- ✓ Rubber bands
- ✓ Scissors
- ✓ Stapler
- ✓ Tape measure

- ✓ Garbage bags
- ✓ Knife (carton knife)
- ✓ Latex gloves
- ✓ Pencils/pens
- ✓ Pliers
- ✓ Rubber mallet
- ✓ Screwdrivers
- ✓ Stapler remover
- ✓ Ziploc bags of various sizes

Paper Management Systems

- ✓ Bankers boxes
- ✓ File labels
- ✓ Filing system sample
- ✓ Hanging file folders
- ✓ Manila file folders
- ✓ Plastic file storage boxes
- ✓ Post-it notes

Closet System Tools

- ✓ Center punch
- ✓ Drill and Phillips bit
- ✓ Level
- ✓ Wall anchors

📄 ACTIONS

☐ Make a list of resources (handyperson, painter, house cleaner, etc.).

☐ Assemble your tool kit.

Chapter 6

Determine Legal and Insurance Needs

Description: This is one of the most critical decisions you will make as a business owner. This chapter will explain the different business entities and help you choose the right one for your situation and goals. The business entities and their advantages and disadvantages that will be discussed are:

- Sole proprietorship

- General partnership

- Limited liability company (LLC)

- Corporation

- S Corporation

Also discussed in this chapter is how to register with your state and the federal governments, getting insurance for your business, and obtaining licensing.

Disclaimer: This book is intended to provide guidance in regard to the subject matter covered. It is provided with the understanding that the author is not herein engaged in rendering legal, accounting, tax, or marketing professional services. If such services are required, professional assistance should be sought.

REGISTERING WITH STATE AND FEDERAL GOVERNMENTS

To protect your chosen company name, you need to register your company name with the state and federal governments. Also, you protect your personal identity with an EIN. Obtain an Employer Identification Number (EIN) at www.irs.gov/pub/irs-pdf/fss4.pdf by completing the SS-4 Form "Application for Employer Identification Number". There is no cost associated with this application as of this writing.

Registering with your state is done at the state business registry office. For example, in Oregon, register you business at www.filinginoregon.com.

Individuals and Sole Proprietors would file: "Assumed Business Name–New Registration" with the state and include $50 (Oregon) for processing fees and an annual renewal of $50.

Limited Liability Companies (LLCs) would file "Articles of Organization–Limited Liability Company" with the state and include $50 (Oregon) for processing fees (varies by state). Annual renewal of $50 (varies by state).

INSURANCE

While business insurance is not generally required, it's a good idea to purchase enough insurance to cover your company's assets. Even if you form a corporation or an LLC, which shields your personal assets from business liabilities, you still risk losing your business if disaster strikes. Insurance can greatly reduce this risk. The two most common and generally useful types of business insurance policies are property insurance and liability insurance. Remember, as a member of NAPO (www.napo.net) Travelers Insurance Company has agreed to include $10,000 of coverage for "care, custody, and control." If an item is damaged or destroyed while you are responsible for it, you will be covered up to the business property limit of the policy after your deductible is met. In many cases, there is no additional cost for this coverage and it will be automatically included in the basic policy premium of $500–$800 in most states. Travelers also offers bonding coverage for any NAPO member. The fidelity bond will include the business owner and up to three employees. $10,000 of protection can be secured for an annual premium of $120 as of this writing.

PERMITS AND LICENSING

Check with your local (city, county, etc.) jurisdictions for what may be required.

WHAT GOES INTO SELECTING YOUR CHOICE OF BUSINESS ENTITY?

Formalities and Expense in Establishing

Sole proprietorships and partnerships are easy to set up. You don't have to file any special forms or pay any fees to start your business. Plus, they don't require you to follow any special operating rules. However, the personal liability risks can outweigh the ease of establishing these entities.

To form an LLC or corporation, you must file a document with the state and pay a fee, which ranges from about $40–$800, depending on the state where you form your business. Corporations are the most cumbersome to maintain, including electing officers (usually a president, vice president, and secretary) to run the company, and they must keep records of important business decisions and follow other formalities.

Risks and Liabilities

Choosing the right business entity for your business depends largely on the type of services or products it will provide. Even if your business doesn't engage in risky activities for example, trading stocks or repairing roofs, you'll almost surely want to obtain liability insurance and form a business entity that provides personal liability protection, which shields your personal assets from business debts and claims. This means setting up a corporation or a limited liability company (LLC).

Income Taxes

When it comes to taxes, sole proprietorships, partnerships, LLCs, and S Corporations come out about even. These business types are "pass-through" tax entities, which means that all of the profits and losses pass through the business to the owners, who report their share of the profits (or deduct their share of the losses) on their personal income tax returns.

Unlike other business owners, the owners of a regular corporation do not report their shares of corporate profits on their personal tax returns. The owners pay taxes only on profits paid out to them in the form of salaries, bonuses, and dividends.

SOLE PROPRIETORSHIP

A sole proprietorship is a business that is owned by *one* person.

Advantages

This is the simplest of business structures to establish and maintain, but you still need to comply with local registration, business license, or permit laws to make your business legitimate. Unlike an LLC or a corporation, you generally don't have to file any special forms or pay any fees to start working as a sole proprietor. All you have to do is declare your business to be a sole proprietorship when you complete the general registration requirements that apply to all new businesses.

In the eyes of the law, a sole proprietorship is not legally separate from the person who owns it. The fact that a sole proprietorship and its owner are one and the same means that a sole proprietor simply reports all business income or losses on his or her individual income tax return, IRS Form 1040 with Schedule C attached. Most cities and many counties require businesses, even tiny home-based sole proprietorships, to register with them and pay at least a minimum tax. In return, your business will receive a business license or tax registration certificate. If you have employees, you need to obtain an employer identification number from the IRS (otherwise your social security number is your employer identification number).

Disadvantages

You are personally responsible for paying both income taxes and business debts. That means that if your business doesn't pay a supplier, defaults on a debt, or loses a lawsuit, the creditor can legally come after your personal property and savings.

As a sole proprietor, you'll have to take responsibility for withholding and paying all income taxes, something an employer would normally do for you. This means paying a "self-employment" tax, which consists of contributions to Social Security and Medicare, and making payments of estimated taxes throughout the year.

General Partnership

Advantages

You don't have to file any paperwork to establish a general partnership; just agreeing to go into business with another person will get you started. Of course, partnerships must fulfill the same local registration requirements as any new business, such as applying for a business license. Most cities require businesses to register with them and pay at least a minimum tax. You may also have to obtain an employer identification number from the IRS.

Again, the IRS does not consider partnerships to be separate from their owners for tax purposes. Instead, they are considered "pass-through" tax entities. This means that all of the profits and losses of the partnership "pass through" the business to the partners, who pay taxes on their share of the profits (or deduct their share of the losses) on their individual income tax returns. Each partner's share of profits and losses should be set out in a written partnership agreement.

Disadvantages

Partners are personally liable for all business debts and obligations, including court judgments. This means that if the business itself can't pay a creditor, such as a supplier, lender, or landlord, the creditor can legally come after any partner's house, car, or other possessions.

Corporation

A corporation is an independent legal entity, separate from the people who own, control, and manage it. In other words, corporation and tax laws view the corporation as a legal "person," meaning that the corporation can enter into contracts, incur debts, and pay taxes apart from its owners. A corporation does not dissolve when its owners (shareholders) change or die. The owners of a corporation are not personally responsible for the corporation's debts; this is called limited liability.

Advantages

One of the main advantages of incorporating is that the owners' personal assets are protected from creditors of the corporation. For instance, if a court judgment is entered against your corporation saying that it owes a creditor $50,000, normally, you can't be forced to use personal assets, such as your house, to pay the debt. Because only corporate assets need be used to pay business debts, you stand to lose only the money that you've invested in the corporation.

Disadvantages

To form a corporation, you must file articles of incorporation with the state corporations division. Filing fees are minimal. For example, Oregon's filing fee is $20.

In addition to filing articles of incorporation, you must create corporate bylaws. While bylaws do not have to be filed with the state, they are important because they set out the basic rules that govern the ongoing formalities and decisions of corporate life, such as how and when to hold regular and special meetings of directors and shareholders and the number of votes that are necessary to approve corporate decisions.

Finally, you must issue stock certificates to the initial owners (shareholders) of the corporation and record who owns the ownership interests (shares or stock) in the business.

Corporations and their owners must observe certain formalities to retain the corporation's status as a separate entity. Specifically, corporations must:

- Hold annual shareholders' and directors' meetings.

- Keep minutes of shareholders' and directors' major decisions.

- Make sure that corporate officers and directors sign documents in the name of the corporation.

- Maintain separate bank accounts from their owners.

- Keep detailed financial records.

- File a separate corporate income tax return

S CORPORATION

An S corporation is a regular corporation that has elected "S corporation" tax status. An S corporation lets you enjoy the limited liability of a corporate shareholder but pay income taxes on the same basis as a sole proprietor, partner, or LLC.

Advantages

Owners have limited personal liability for business debts. Owners report their share of corporate profit or loss on their personal tax returns. Owners can use corporate loss to offset income from other sources. Fringe benefits can be deducted as business expense.

Disadvantages

It is more expensive to create than a partnership or sole proprietorship. There is more paperwork than for a limited liability company, which offers similar advantages. The income must be allocated to owners according to their ownership interests. The fringe benefits are limited for owners who own more than 2 percent of shares.

LIMITED LIABILITY COMPANY (LLC)

A limited liability company (LLC) is an ownership structure that is similar to a corporation. Actually, it combines attributes of both corporations and partnerships (or, for one-person LLCs, sole proprietorships). An LLC offers the corporation protection from personal liability for business debts and the pass-through tax structure of partnerships and sole proprietorships. If you're concerned about being held personally liable for debts of your business, then an LLC may be just the thing for you.

Advantages

While LLC owners enjoy limited personal liability for many of their business transactions, it is important to realize that this protection is not absolute. This drawback is not unique to LLCs; however, the same exceptions apply to corporations. An LLC owner can be held personally liable if he or she:

- Personally and directly injures someone

- Personally guarantees a bank loan or a business debt on which the LLC defaults

- Fails to deposit taxes withheld from employees' wages

- Intentionally does something fraudulent, illegal, or clearly wrong-headed that causes harm to the company or to someone else

- Treats the LLC as an extension of his or her personal affairs, rather than as a separate legal entity

This last exception is the most important. In some circumstances, a court might say that the LLC doesn't really exist and find that its owners are really doing business as individuals, who are personally liable for their acts. To keep this from happening, make sure you and your co-owners:

- Act fairly and legally. Do not conceal or misrepresent material facts or the state of your finances to vendors, creditors, or other outsiders.

- Fund your LLC adequately. Invest enough cash into the business so that your LLC can meet foreseeable expenses and liabilities.

- Keep LLC and personal business separate. Get a federal employer identification number, open up a business-only checking account, and keep your personal finances out of your LLC accounting books.

- Create an operating agreement. Having a formal written operating agreement lends credibility to your LLCs separate existence.

- Always use and state LLC with your business name.

To create an LLC, you begin by filing articles of organization (in some states called a certificate of organization or certificate of formation) with the LLC division of your state government. This office is often in the same department as the corporations division, which is usually part of the secretary of state's office. Filing fees are typically $100 or less (for example, in Oregon, the filing fee is $50).

You can now form an LLC with just one person. While there's no maximum number of owners that an LLC can have, for practical reasons, you'll probably want to keep the group small. An LLC that's actively owned and operated by more than about five people risks problems with maintaining good communication and reaching consensus among the owners.

Many states supply a blank one-page form for the articles of organization, on which you need only specify a few basic details about your LLC, such as its name and address and contact information for a person involved with the LLC (usually called a registered agent) who will receive legal papers on its behalf. Some states also require you to list the names and addresses of the LLC members.

In addition to filing articles of organization, you must create a written LLC operating agreement. While you don't have to file your operating agreement with the state, it's a crucial document because it sets out the LLC members' rights and responsibilities, their percentage interests in the business, and their share of the profits.

Finally, your LLC must fulfill the same local registration requirements as any new business, such as applying for a business license and registering a fictitious or assumed business name.

Disadvantages

It is more expensive to create than a partnership or sole proprietorship because of the attorney fees associated with the preparation of the entity's documents.

🗎 ACTIONS

☐ Meet with your accountant and attorney to determine which business entity you should form based on your business model.

☐ After you have your business name (read Chapter 7 first) register your business with the states you will be doing business in.

☐ After you have your business name and business entity documents (articles of incorporation or articles of organization) complete the federal SS-4 form to obtain an EIN number).

☐ After you have your EIN number obtain a business checking account.

☐ After you have your business name apply for business license.

Chapter 7

Name and Register Your Business for Maximum Impact

Description: People make an impression in the first two seconds they meet someone. If your name is the first way to introduce yourself to a prospective client, what impression will you make?

- What's in a name?

- What do you want to project?

- What first impression do you want to make?

- How to search for business names

- How to search for Internet domain names

- How to register your business name

WHAT'S IN A NAME?

It is how you are viewed by anyone who reads it. They get an instant image of your business and what you do.

What Do You Want to Project?

You want your name to project that you are professional and qualified. What other qualities should it indicate?

First Impressions Do Matter

People get an impression of you within the first two seconds of meeting you. If your business name is their first impression, you need to consider including in your business name information about what you do as a professional organizer.

Be Careful Using Your Own Personal Name

Names that don't work well because they don't indicate they are in the professional organizing business include:

- All Bright Ideas (Diane Albright)
- Andrews Personal Consulting (Sandra Andrews)
- Busy as a Bea (Bea Baird)
- Ideas in Bloom (Wendy Bloom)
- Options by Ana (Ana Popielnicki)

Names that do work because they indicate the person is a professional organizer include:

- Organized by Noon (Lisa Noon)
- Organize with Kate (Kate Murrell)

- Cheryl's Organizing Concepts (Cheryl Larson)
- Organization by Suzanne (Suzanne Hosea)

More names that do not indicate you are a professional organizer include:

- A Custom Solution
- A to Z Home Management
- Getting Clear
- Timely Living
- Clear the Decks
- Winged Pig

Names that are too cute or misuse words include:

- Organique-Unique
- H/OME (Home/Office Made Easy)
- De-Clutter Bug
- Mind Over Matter (MOM)

Names that indicate exactly what you do include:

- Office Organizers of Houston
- Creative Organizing Solutions
- The Organizing Coach

- Organizing Solutions

- Organizing Resources

Choose Your Name Wisely

Every time you change your name, you will need to register the new name with the state business registry. You may also incur the expense of reprinting business cards and other promotional and marketing pieces.

Register Your Business Name

- Web site domain name registration: Check www.whois.net, www.godaddy.com, or www.networksolutions.com to search if your name is available.

- State business registry: For example, in Oregon go to www.filinginoregon.com.

- Federal registration: Register at www.uspto.gov. This is the U.S. Patent and Trademark Office.

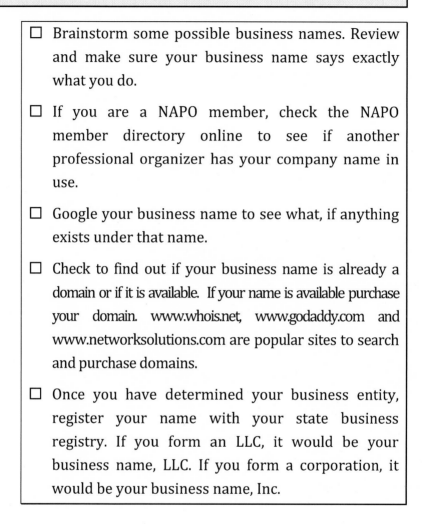

📄**ACTIONS**

☐ Brainstorm some possible business names. Review and make sure your business name says exactly what you do.

☐ If you are a NAPO member, check the NAPO member directory online to see if another professional organizer has your company name in use.

☐ Google your business name to see what, if anything exists under that name.

☐ Check to find out if your business name is already a domain or if it is available. If your name is available purchase your domain. www.whois.net, www.godaddy.com and www.networksolutions.com are popular sites to search and purchase domains.

☐ Once you have determined your business entity, register your name with your state business registry. If you form an LLC, it would be your business name, LLC. If you form a corporation, it would be your business name, Inc.

Chapter 8

Tax Issues to Consider and Understand: What You Need to Know to Be Tax Savvy and Tax Benefits You Should Understand

Description: This chapter will guide you through the labyrinth of tax details a small and home business owner needs to understand and comply with including:

- Selecting software to track you business records
- Deductions for you home business
- Business use of your home
- Business use of your automobile
- Business travel
- Family members as employees
- Estimated taxes
- Payroll taxes
- Local taxes and licenses
- Filing form 1099 for professional services
- Retirement plans

Disclaimer: This book is intended to provide guidance in regard to the subject matter covered. It is provided with the understanding that the author is not herein engaged in rendering legal, accounting, tax, or marketing professional services. If such services are required, professional assistance should be sought.

Note: Source of information for this chapter is Julia Fitzgerald, CPA, Portland, Oregon. Unless otherwise noted, the information in this chapter is effective as of this writing and subject to change.

SOFTWARE OPTIONS FOR YOUR BUSINESS RECORDS

- Quicken Deluxe

- Quicken Premier

- Quicken Premier Home & Business

- QuickBooks Online

- QuickBooks Simple Start

- QuickBooks Pro

- QuickBooks Premier

- QuickBooks for Specific Industries

- Web site www.intuit.com

TIPS ON SETTING UP QUICKEN OR QUICKBOOKS

- Set up the Category/Account list according to your needs (the shorter the better).

- Set up your filing system according to your Category/Account names.

- Code transactions consistently.

- Ask questions from an expert.

- Get training if you have never used financial accounting software.

- Reconcile your bank and credit card statements monthly.

- Reconcile your accounts receivable and payables monthly.

- Learn one module at a time.

- If you work with an accountant, have them set-up your category/account names. It will save you time and money when they prepare your tax filing.

DEDUCTIONS FOR YOUR BUSINESS

- Advertising

- Car and truck expenses: Actual vs. mileage

- Commissions and fees: Services for non-employees you must send a 1099 for payments of $600 or more to the same recipient.

- Depreciation: Up to $250,000 on new equipment purchased each year.

- Insurance: Liability, malpractice, casualty, overhead, bonds, merchandise and inventory, workers compensation.

- Health insurance: Can deduct 100 percent if you are not eligible for coverage with a group health plan.

- Interest expense on business note payables

- Legal and professional fees

- Office expenses

- Pension and profit-sharing plans

- Rent or lease

- Repairs and maintenance

- Supplies

- Taxes and licenses

- Training and education

- Travel

- Meals and entertainment

- Utilities

- Telephone

- Wages

- Professional dues and memberships (except health clubs)

- Other expenses

Asset Versus Expense

Classify business equipment and furnishings as an asset if it has a life longer than one year and costs greater than $200; otherwise classify as supplies expense. The cost to place the equipment into use is included in the cost, that is, shipping, labor to install etc.

BUSINESS USE OF HOME

The business percentages of expenses below are generally deductible on Form 8829:

- Mortgage interest

- Real estate taxes

- Home repairs and maintenance

- Water, sewer, garbage

- Rent

- Utilities (first home line not deductible)

- Depreciation

- House insurance

- Security system

- Casualty losses

Note: Lawn care/landscaping expenses are not deductible

Business Percentage

Business percentage of the home is determined by dividing the area exclusively used for business by the total area of the home.

- Direct expense: Benefit only the business part of the home. 100 percent of direct expenses are generally deductible against business income.

- Indirect expense: Benefit both the business and personal parts of the home. Included are the upkeep and running of the entire home. The business percentages of indirect expenses are generally deductible against business income.

- It is not always the best option to claim a home office for tax purposes. Ask your accountant what is best for your situation.

Sale of the Home

For sales of a personal residence, a homeowner may exclude from income up to $250,000 of gain, and a married couple may exclude up to $500,000 of gain realized on the sale.

Individuals

- Ownership and use: The individual must have owned and used the home as a principal residence for at least two out of the five years prior to the sale (the two years do not have to be consecutive).

- Frequency limitation: The exclusion applies to only one sale every two years.

Married Couples

- Joint return: The married couple must file a joint return.

- Ownership: Either or both spouses must have owned the residence for at least two out of the five years prior to the sale.

- Use: Both spouses must have used the residence as their principal residence for at least two out of the five years prior to the sale.

- Frequency limitation: Neither spouse may have sold a home more than once every two years.

BUSINESS USE OF AUTOMOBILE

- Actual costs: Deduct the business-use percentage times the actual cost of running the vehicle (gas, oil, repairs, insurance, tires, license, etc.)

- Standard mileage: Deduct the standard mileage rate (55 cents as of January 9, 2009), which includes all vehicle costs except business parking and tolls, the business percentage of interest paid on a vehicle loan, and the business percentage of personal property taxes paid on the vehicle. Depreciation is included in the cents per mile deduction.

BUSINESS TRAVEL

Elements to prove business travel expenses include:

- Amount: Amount of each separate expense for travel, lodging and meals.

- Time: Date left and returned for trip and number of days for business.

- Place: Name of city or other designation.

- Business Purpose: Business reason for travel or the business benefit gained or expected to be gained.

Deductibility of travel expenses include:

- Transportation and lodging : 100 percent

- Meals while away from home: 50 percent

- Cost of conference/seminar : 100 percent

Types of expenditures include:

- Transportation: Travel by airplane, train, bus, or car between home and business destination. If the ticket is provided or free as a result of a frequent traveler or similar program, the cost is zero.

- Commuter bus, taxi, airport limousine: Fares for transportation to or from airport or station and the hotel, and hotel and location of the business meeting place.

- Car: Operating and maintaining a car when traveling away from home on business. Deduct actual expenses or the standard mileage rate, including business-related tolls and parking.

- Lodging and meals: Lodging and meals if the business trip is overnight or long enough to require a stop for sleep. Cost of meals includes amounts spent for food, beverages, taxes, and related tips.

- Cleaning: Dry cleaning and laundry.

- Telephone: Business calls on a business trip. Includes business communication by fax machine or other communication devices.

BUSINESS VERSUS PERSONAL TRAVEL EXPENSES

- Entirely for business: All travel expenses are deductible.

- Primarily for business: Deductible travel expenses include the travel costs of getting to and from the business destination, and any business-related expenses at the business destination. (Nonbusiness side trips are not deductible.) Whether a trip is primarily business or personal depends on the facts and circumstances of each case. The amount of time during the trip spent on personal activity compared to the amount of time spent on activities directly relating to business is an important factor in determining whether the trip is primarily personal.

- Primarily for personal reasons: The entire cost of the trip is nondeductible. However, any business-related expenses incurred at the destination are deductible.

FAMILY MEMBERS AS EMPLOYEES

Sole Proprietors Can Deduct Cost of Medical Expenses Paid to Employee-Spouse

Under an accident and health plan that meets the requirements of Section 105(b) sole proprietors can deduct as business expenses the full amount of medical reimbursement costs paid to employees.

If the sole proprietor's spouse is an employee, the sole proprietor can be covered under the spouse's medical plan since the sole proprietor is part of the employee's family.

Regulations

- A written agreement must be in place before a medical reimbursement plan can be implemented.

- An employee-spouse must actually perform services for the employer. The IRS is likely to reclassify amounts paid to an employee-spouse if it determines that the spouse did not function as a bona fide employee.

Hire Children to Save Tax

An employer-parent can reduce self-employment income from taxation by hiring his or her child.

- Wages are exempt for FICA taxes for a child under age eighteen if employed in a parent's unincorporated business.

- A dependent's standard deduction can be up to $5,450 if all income is earned income.

- A child may be eligible to contribute up to $5,000 to a deductible IRA.

- Wages paid by a parent to a child are deductible by the parent's business if:

- Work is done in connection with the parent's trade or business.

- The child actually performs the work for which wages are paid.

- Payments are actually made.

Therefore, by hiring your child, you can reduce self-employment income by $10,450 which will ultimately reduce self-employment taxes.

ESTIMATED TAXES

The general rule for estimated tax payments is to pay in 100 percent of last year's total tax or 90 percent of this year's total tax. Divide the total into four payments to be paid each quarter by the due date.

- April 15–1st payment due.

- June 15–2nd payment due.

- September 15–3rd payment due.

- January 15–4th payment due.

To electronically pay all your taxes, go to www.eftps.gov and enroll. Pay your taxes more often than four times. For cash flow, pay something each month toward your estimated taxes.

PAYROLL TAXES

Federal Forms
- Form 941 Employers Quarterly Federal Tax Return: Due each quarter by the end of the month following the quarter (e.g., 1st quarter due by April 30).

- Form 940 Employers: Due by January 30 for the previous year's payroll.

- Form 944 Employers Annual Federal Tax Return: Due by January 31st for the previous year's payroll.

- Form W-2 Employee Wage statements: Due to recipients by January 30 for the previous year's payroll.

- Form 1099 Misc.: Due to the recipients by January 30 for the previous year's non-employee compensation. Must send one to each unincorporated individual or business for payments of $600 or greater.

State Forms (Oregon as an example)
- Form OQ Oregon Combined Quarterly Tax Report: Due each quarter by the end of the month following the quarter.

- Form WR Oregon Annual Withholding Tax Reconciliation Report.

Local Taxes (Oregon as an example)
- Personal Property Tax: Due March 1 of each year for previous calendar year. Tax is paid on value of equipment and furniture that business has accumulated since inception. As of this writing, no tax paid for assets valued less than $14,000.

- TriMet and LTD Transit District Self-Employment Taxes (Oregon): Due April 15 of each year. This income tax is applied to self-employment earnings of taxpayers doing business, or providing services, within the district that are not subject to payroll tax.

- Combined Report Form (Oregon): Portland City Business License-Multnomah County Business Income Tax. City rate 2.2 percent of net income. Minimum $100.00 annually. County Rate 1.45 percent of net income. Minimum $100.00 annually. Required to file this form when your gross receipts equal or exceed $50,000. The Portland, Oregon Bureau of Licenses Web site is www.pdxbl.org.

Filing Form 1099

Form 1099-Misc is required to be filed for each person the business pays professional fees of $600 or more in a calendar year. The 1099s must be furnished to the recipients by February 1 of each year for the previous calendar year's activity. A Form 1096 must accompany the 1099 that is sent to the government.

RETIREMENT OPTIONS FOR SINGLE-OWNER SELF-EMPLOYED SMALL BUSINESS

- Traditional IRA: Must have earned income and not be seventy and a half years old by the end of the year. Contribute up to $5,000, if age fifty or over contribute up to $6,000. All distributions are taxable.

- Roth IRA: Must have earned income. May be of any age. Contributions will decrease for married-filing-joint incomes of $159,000–$169,000. Single and head of household filers making $101,000–$116,000. No tax deduction allowed. Contribute up to $5,000, if age fifty or over contribute up to $6,000.

- SEP-IRA or Single 401(k): Anyone with self-employment income. Contributions are treated the same as IRAs. Contribute up to 20 percent of net self-employment income after self-employment tax. Maximum of $46,000.

- Simple IRA can contribute up to $10,500, if age fifty or over contribute up to $13,000.

REFERENCED FORMS

- Articles of Organization—Limited Liability Company

- Assumed Business Name —New Registration

- SS-4 Online Application for Employer Identification Number

- Schedule C Profit or Loss From Business

- 1040ES Vouchers

- 940-EZ Employer's Annual Federal Unemployment Tax Return

- 941 Employer's Quarterly Federal Tax Return

- 944 Employer's Annual Federal Tax Return

- W-4 Employee's Withholding Allowance Certificate (required to fill out annually)

- City of Portland Oregon Bureau of Licenses Application

- Combined Report Form—Portland Business License—Multnomah County Business Income Tax

- Listing of Surrounding area local taxes

- TriMet Self-Employment Tax form

- Form 1099-Misc

📄 ACTIONS

☐ Select and set-up software or other financial recordkeeping system to track income and deductions for your business.

☐ Select and set-up a payroll service for your business.

☐ Decide if you will use actual costs or standard mileage for business use of automobile.

☐ Complete appropriate referenced forms for your business model and entity.

Chapter 9

Marketing and Branding Your Organizing Business

Description: This chapter covers how to create a brand for yourself, how to create a winning marketing message and successful marketing approaches, how to develop your network for long-term success, and how to create a successful Web site.

- Creating your brand

- Writing a winning marketing message

- Communicating your value

- Creating your elevator speech

- Developing your network of strategic alliances

- Developing a successful Web site

- Five steps to creating a blog with Google

- Thirty-minute formula

- One hundred marketing approaches

WHAT IS THE DIFFERENCE BETWEEN MARKETING, ADVERTISING, AND PUBLIC RELATIONS?

If the circus is coming to town, and you paint a sign saying, "Circus coming to the fairgrounds Saturday," that's *advertising*. If you put the sign on the back of an elephant and walk him into town, that's *promotion*. If the elephant walks through the mayor's flowerbed, that's *publicity*. If you can get the mayor to laugh about it, that's *public relations*, and if you actually planned the elephant's walk, that's *marketing*.

CREATING YOUR BRAND

A brand is more than a logo. A brand means being known. A brand is recognition. You want clients to recognize, respond, and remember you! A brand is the promise of an experience. Your brand should include what experience you want your clients to have with you. Refer to the benefits (value) you provide your clients:

- Empowered

- In control

- Attain goals

- Achievable results

- Peace of mind

- More time

- Fun

- Simple

You need to capitalize on *your* strengths. What is *your* promise of an experience?

For example, with SolutionsForYou—I have the solutions, I can solve their problems, and I am confident that I can provide solutions that will work for them.

It is not a brand unless it is remarkable. You must stand out from everyone else in your line of business. How will you stand out from your competitors?

WRITING A WINNING MARKETING MESSAGE AND COMMUNICATING YOUR VALUE

A marketing message is comprised of five elements:

1. Positioning idea: Your key marketing message. It is similar to a tagline.

2. Position description: Expansion of your marketing message. It is similar to your mission statement.

3. Key messages: No more than three. Pull them from your position description.

4. Supporting details: Expansion of your key messages.

5. Key benefits: What your client gains (the value/benefits you give them).

Here is an example of a marketing message:

Professional Organizer Training Institute™ Marketing Message

Positioning Idea	The global market leader in Professional Organizer Business Owner Training.		
Positioning Description	Professional Organizer Training Institute™ is the leading global provider of <u>both business development and professional organizer client engagement training</u> that enable Professional Organizers to attract their key client, increase their confidence, and manage their business through the knowledge, skills, systems, tools, expertise, experience, and continuous support provided by Certified Professional Organizers® via live seminars, state-of-the-art webinars, or individual coaching, mentoring, and self-study.		
Key Messages	**Attract more key clients** Learn how to develop a marketing message and plan to attract your key client.	**Manage your PO business** Provide the tools and expertise for participants to successfully start, run and manage a business specific to the Professional Organizer industry.	**Multiple Training Venues** Provide the knowledge, skills, systems, tools, experience, certification, and continuous support needed to work with clients specific to the Professional organizer industry from anywhere in the world.
Supporting Details	• Introduction and awareness of key client and specialized services • Identification of key client and services • Research and write a business plan supporting key client market • Marketing and branding methodology and techniques to attract key client • Tools and support (web development) to market participants business to their key client	• Understanding the Professional Organizer Industry Associations and Credentials • Provide a detailed Action Plan and mentoring to implement participants Professional Organizer Business • Provide tax, legal and insurance knowledge to the Professional Organizer Industry	• Live Seminar with hands-on client practicum, certification, and continuous support • State-of-the art Webinar training with continuous support • Individual coaching , mentoring and self-study
Key Benefits	**Business is positioned in the market to attract key client**	**Positioned for stability and growth**	**Continuous Training is financially and geographically achievable**

CREATING YOUR ELEVATOR SPEECH

Why do you need one? It is your answer to, "What do you do?" You want a clear, concise, and valuable message. This is your chance to attract potential clients and stand out from your competitors. Who needs your services and are you talking to them? You want to be perceived as credible, competent, and professional. You want to be remembered, so don't be boring.

The Formula

Keep it short–seven to ten words. Elements to include when creating your own speech include:

1. What you do

2. Who you serve

3. What your clients *need*

4. What your clients really *want*

Example
I help families solve their organizing challenges.
1. What I do: I help

2. Who I serve: families

3. What my clients need: solutions

4. What my clients want: to be organized

Now when they say, "Tell me more," you need to be able to explain the details of what you do. Now it is about you and how you can provide the solutions they need. Prepare a follow-up to your elevator speech for various audiences.

DEVELOPING YOUR NETWORK OF STRATEGIC ALLIANCES

Strategic alliances are individuals or businesses who share similar clients with you. Network every day. Talk to everyone about your business. Who do you know that can help you promote your business? Who can you partner with and strategically align yourself with to provide mutual marketing opportunities?

Strategic alliance examples include:

- Realtors

- Interior designers

- Schools

- Doctors

- Lawyers

- Certified public accountants

- Retirement facilities (elderly)

- Financial investment representatives

- Feng Shui consultants

- Wardrobe consultants

- Cleaning services

- Networking groups

DEVELOPING A SUCCESSFUL WEB SITE

Websites generally consist of the following pages:

- Home: Where you communicate to your ideal client your marketing message.

- About Us: A bio about you. Your background, how you became a professional organizer, your education and training, your organizing philosophy, your credentials and memberships.

- Contact: Your company phone number, e-mail, needs assessment form.

- Services: What you will provide and what the client will receive (value and benefits).

Additional pages might consist of:

- Approach: How to work with a professional organizer.

- Before/After Pictures: Samples of client projects. Include how long it took both your time and client time, materials used and cost and resources for, what their before state was, what their goals were, what the outcome is.

- Resources: A listing of services that your clients can benefit from (i.e., your strategic alliances, donation resources, product resources, etc.).

- Newsletter or blog.

- Frequently Asked Questions (FAQs).

Include in your design your company colors, logo, tagline, and font as they all communicate your brand.

Other information to disclose might include:

- Privacy statement

- Webmaster information or link to their Web site

- Copyright protection ©

Ways to optimize your Web site include:

- Submitting to search engines (Google, Yahoo, MSN, etc.)

- Adding key words: Google AdWords Keyword Tool is free, and it tells you how many people are searching for each keyword phrase as well as the level of competition.

Some examples of key words you might include are: professional organizer, your city, your state, company name, organizing services, residential organizing, and business organizing. To locate a Web site's title, key words, description, and other coding information, right click on the Web site page and select "view source".

- Description: What appears with your Web site listing when someone does a search for related terms in a search engine. For example, the description for the home page of the Professional Organizer Training Institute Web site is: Professional Organizer Training Institute™: Offering you a choice of professional organizer training programs (seminar, webinar, and self-study) developed and delivered by Certified Professional Organizers.

Professional Organizer Training Programs - The **Professional ...**
Professional Organizer Training Institute™: Offering you a choice of **professional organizer training** programs (seminar, webinar and self-study) developed ...
www.professionalorganizertraininginstitute.com/ - 46k - Cached - Similar pages

FIVE STEPS TO CREATING A BLOG WITH GOOGLE

A blog is a communication medium for you to communicate with clients and prospective clients on an ongoing basis. This is different than a newsletter you distribute on a reoccurring or regular basis. You can provide organizing tips, inspiration, resources, and anything else that will provide value to your key clients—thereby increasing your value. For an example, visit www.solutionsforyouorganizing.blogspot.com.

A blog is very easy to create with Google. Follow these steps:

1. Create a Google account. Go to www.Google.com. Sign in if you have a Google account. Otherwise create a Google account. Select "blogger."

2. Name your blog.

3. Choose a template. You can easily change your template any time.

4. Adjust your settings and layout. This is where you format how your blog page will appear and what access you give. Including:

   · Page elements

   · Font and colors

   · Edit HTML

   · Edit template

   · Change title

   · Add description

   · Add your blog to Google's listings

   · Let search engines find your blog

   · Show quick editing on your blog

   · Show email post links

5. Post a blog entry.

THIRTY-MINUTE MARKETING FORMULA (SOURCE WWW.VERONIKANOIZE.COM FREE REPORT: HOW TO DOUBLE YOUR BUSINESS IN 30 DAYS)

Every day spend the first thirty minutes:

1. Reviewing your marketing plan

2. Reviewing your financials

3. Looking at your calendar. Is it moving you forward? Is it full? If not, what can you do to generate business?

4. Focusing on your business and getting inspiration

5. Brainstorming

6. Reading an article about organizing or running a business

7. Making five good karma calls just to say, "Hello, I'm thinking of you" or to compliment someone. The point is to connect with people because *marketing is relationships.*

TOP TEN MARKETING APPROACHES

1. Web site—www.godaddy.com

2. Business cards—www.prstore.com

3. Flyers

4. Brochures—www.prstore.com

5. Newsletter (see handouts for monthly examples)

There are a variety of ways you can create and distribute your newsletter. Some common methods are:

- Send your newsletter with www.constantcontact.com.

- For a more professional look and feel than a Word document, create your newsletter using Microsoft Publisher and attach it to an e-mail in pdf format. You can use www.primopdf.com for creating a free pdf.

- Blog

- U.S. Postal Service

- Content Ideas:

- Introduction: A theme for the month. Such as Back to School Organizing for the September newsletter.

- Tip of the month

- Featured product

- Client success story: Feature one of your client projects along with before/after pictures.

- Featured professional resource: Feature one of your strategic alliances and how they can help your clients.

6. Give a presentation on topics such as time, paper, and space management (see Chapters 15, 16, and 17 for content ideas).

7. Gift certificates

8. Sign on your car www.fastsigns.com

9. Silent auctions

10. Send seasonal greeting cards www.sendoutcards.com

ONE HUNDRED MARKETING APPROACHES (SOURCE: WWW.VICKYSVIRTUALOFFICE.COM APRIL 2008 AND REWRITTEN SPECIFICALLY FOR THE PROFESSIONAL ORGANIZER INDUSTRY)

General Ideas

1. Never let a day pass without engaging in at least one marketing activity (see thirty-minute marketing formula).

2. Determine a percentage of gross income to spend annually on marketing.

3. Set specific marketing goals every year. Review and adjust quarterly.

4. Maintain a tickler file of marketing ideas for later use.

5. Carry business cards with you (all day, every day). See www.prstore.com or www.thelogocompany.net.

6. Create a personal nametag or pin with your company name and logo on it and wear it at high-visibility meetings.

Target Market

7. Stay alert to trends that might impact your target market, product, or promotion strategy.

8. Read market research studies about your profession, industry, product, target market groups, etc.

9. Collect competitors' ads and literature. Study them for information about strategy, product features, benefits, etc.

10. Ask clients why they hired you and solicit suggestions for improvement.

11. Ask former clients why they left you.

12. Identify a new market.

13. Join a list-serve (e-mail list) related to your profession. See www.napo.net.

14. Subscribe to a list-serve or blog that serves your target market.

Networking and Word of Mouth

15. Join a chamber of commerce or other organization.

16. Join or organize a breakfast club with other professionals (not in your field) to discuss business and network referrals.

17. Mail a brochure to members of organizations to which you belong.

18. Send letters to attendees after you attend a conference.

19. Join a community list-serve (e-mail list) on the Internet.

Product Development

20. Create a new service, technique, or product.

21. Offer a simpler/cheaper/smaller version of your (or existing) product or service.

22. Offer a fancier/more expensive/faster/bigger version of your (or existing) product or service.

23. Update your services.

Education, Resources, and Information

24. Establish a marketing and public relations advisory and referral team composed of your colleagues and/or neighboring business owners, share ideas and referrals, and discuss community issues. Meet quarterly for breakfast.

25. Attend a marketing seminar.

26. Read a marketing book.

27. Subscribe to a marketing newsletter or other publication.

28. Subscribe to a marketing list-serve on the Internet.

29. Subscribe to a marketing blog on the Internet www.marketing-expert.blogspot.com.

30. Train your clients and colleagues to promote referrals.

31. Hold a monthly marketing meeting with employees or associates to discuss strategy and status and solicit marketing ideas.

32. Join an association or organization related to your profession. See www.napo.net.

33. Get a marketing intern to take you on as a client. It will give the intern experience and you some free marketing help.

34. Maintain a consultant card file for finding designers, writers, and other marketing professionals. Hire a marketing consultant to brainstorm with.

Pricing and Payment

35. Analyze your fee structure and look for areas requiring modifications or adjustments.

36. Establish a credit card payment option for clients. See www.paypal.com.

37. Learn to barter and offer discounts to members of certain clubs/professional groups/organizations in exchange for promotions in their publications.

38. Give quick pay or cash discounts.

39. Offer financing or installment plans.

Marketing Communications

40. Publish a newsletter for customers and prospects (it doesn't have to be fancy or expensive). See www.constantcontact.com.

41. Develop a brochure of services. See www.prstore.com or www.thelogocompany.net.

42. Remember, business cards aren't working for you if they're in the box. Pass them out! Give prospects two business cards and brochures—one to keep and one to pass along.

43. Create a calendar to give away to customers and prospects. See www.prstore.com.

44. Print a tagline and/or one-sentence description of your business on letterhead, fax cover sheets, and invoices.

45. Develop a site on the World Wide Web. See www.godaddy.com or www.INDOedesign.com.

46. Create a signature file to be used for all your e-mail

messages. It should contain contact details, including your Web site address and key information about your company that will make the reader want to contact you.

47. Include testimonials from customers in your literature and on your Web site.

Media Relations

48. Update your media list often so that press releases are sent to the right media outlet and person.

49. Write a column for the local newspaper, local business journal, or trade publication.

50. Publish an article and circulate reprints.

51. Send timely and newsworthy press releases as often as needed.

52. Get public relations and media training or read up on it.

53. Appear on a radio or TV talk show.

54. Write a letter to the editor of your local newspaper or trade magazine.

55. Get a publicity photo taken and enclose with press releases.

56. Consistently review newspapers and magazines for possible PR opportunities.

57. Submit tip articles to newsletters, e-zines (An e-zine is a periodic publication distributed by email or posted on a Web site. E-zines are typically tightly focused on a subject area), and newspapers.

58. Conduct industry research and develop a press release or article to announce an important discovery in your field.

59. Create a media kit and keep its contents current.

Customer Service and Customer Relations

60. Return phone calls promptly.

61. Record a memorable message or tip of the day on your outgoing answering machine or voice mail message.

62. Ask clients what you can do the help them.

63. Take clients out to a ball game, show, or another special event—just send them two tickets with a note. Hold a seminar at your office for clients and prospects.

64. Send handwritten thank-you notes.

65. Send birthday cards and appropriate seasonal greetings. See www.sendoutcards.com.

66. Photocopy interesting articles and send them to clients and prospects with a handwritten FYI note and your business card.

67. Send a book of interest or other appropriate business gift to a client with a handwritten note.

68. Create an area on your Web site specifically for your customers.

Advertising

69. Get a memorable phone number, such as 1-800-ORGANIZ.

70. Provide Rolodex® cards or phone stickers preprinted with your business contact information.

71. Promote your business jointly with other professionals via cooperative direct mail.

72. Advertise in a specialty directory or in the yellow pages.

73. Write an ad in another language to reach the non-English-speaking market. Place the ad in a publication that your market reads, such as in a Hispanic newspaper.

74. Distribute advertising specialty products such as pens, mouse pads, or mugs.

75. Mail bumps—photos, samples, and other innovative items to your prospect list. (A bump is simply anything that makes the mailing envelope bulge and makes the recipient curious about what's in the envelope!)

76. Create a direct-mail list of hot prospects.

77. Consider nontraditional tactics such as bus backs, billboards, and popular Web sites.

78. Consider a vanity automobile tag with your company name. See www.fastsigns.com.

79. Create a friendly bumper sticker for your car.

80. Code your ads and keep records of results to analyze effectiveness.

81. Create a new or improved company logo or recolor the traditional logo.
    See www.prstore.com, www.elogocontest.com, or www.thelogocompany.net.

82. Sponsor and promote a contest or sweepstakes during GO Month (January).

Special Events and Outreach

83. Get a booth at a fair/trade show attended by your target market.

84. Give a speech or volunteer for a career day at a high school.

85. Teach a class or seminar at a local college or adult education center.

86. Sponsor an Adopt-a-Road area in your community to keep roads litter free. People that pass by the area will see your name on the sign announcing your sponsorship.

87. Volunteer your time to a charity or nonprofit organization.

88. Donate your product or service to a charity auction.

89. Appear on a panel at a professional seminar.

90. Write a how-to pamphlet or article for publishing.

91. Produce and distribute an educational CD-ROM or audio/video tape.

92. Publish a book or an e-book. See www.lulu.com.

Sales Ideas

93. Start every day with two cold or follow-up calls.

94. Read newspapers, business journals, and trade publications for new business openings, personnel appointments, and promotion announcements made by

companies. Send your business literature to appropriate individuals and firms.

95. Give your sales literature to your lawyer, accountant, printer, banker, temp agency, office supply salesperson, advertising agency, etc. (Expand your sales force for free!)

96. Follow up on your direct mailings, e-mail messages, and broadcast faxes with a friendly telephone call.

97. Try using the broadcast fax or e-mail delivery methods instead of direct mail. (Broadcast fax and e-mail allows you to send the same message to many locations at once.) See www.constantcontact.com.

98. Use broadcast faxes or e-mail messages to notify your customers of product service updates. See www.constantcontact.com.

99. Extend your hours of operation.

100. Call and/or send mail to former clients to try and reactivate them.

📄 ACTIONS

☐ Write your marketing message.

☐ Write your elevator speech.

☐ Write text for your Web site.

☐ Research other professional organizer Web sites.

☐ Create a blog.

☐ Do at least one of the one hundred marketing ideas each week.

☐ Call five people and practice making karma calls.

Part II: Your Clientele

Chapter 10

Client Process, Initial Client Contact, and Your Thirty-Second Hook

Description: The initial client contact is the first of the five phases of the client process. The thirty-second hook will help prepare you for when a client calls.

Five phases of the client process

- Phase one—initial client contact
  - What to say when a client first calls
  - Developing your thirty-second hook
  - What you *initially* need to know from a client
  - Scheduling your needs assessment consultation

CLIENT PROCESS

The client process consists of five phases; initial client contact, needs assessment consultation/organizing plan of action, scheduling the project, implementation of the project using the 5 Steps to Organizing® process (see Chapter 13), and lastly client follow-up and maintenance.

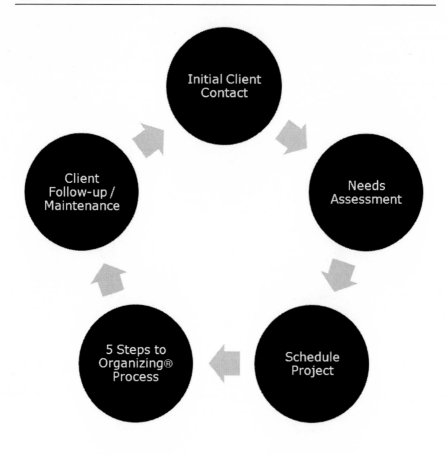

POINTS TO CONSIDER WHEN YOUR CLIENT CALLS

- What is your objective?

- How do you want to be perceived?

- Be professional.

- Have professional-sounding voice mail message.

- Train your family members to answer your phone or have a separate phone line for your business.

- Would you want to work with you after hearing you talk?

DEVELOPING YOUR THIRTY-SECOND HOOK

You must be prepared to succinctly talk about your business and how you can help the client. Your hook should include the following:

- Your fees

- Confidential services

- Your credibility

- How you work or your process

- Benefits of working with you

Example

You can expect complete confidentiality, and I adhere to the National Association of Professional Organizers code of ethics. I work with my clients in three phases.

The first phase is a complimentary needs assessment to define your goals and schedule organizing sessions for the second phase. The second phase is the implementation of my organizing process. My rate for phase two sessions is $X/hour. The implementation can be accomplished by working with you hands-on providing side-by-side assistance. Or, I can work with you by coaching, providing you with assignments to complete on your own between our consultations. The third phase is a thirty-minute complimentary evaluation appointment to insure your organizing systems are working for you.

The benefits you will receive from my services might include more time and space, saving money, improved relationships, less stress, and increased productivity and focus. Doesn't that sound great?

When is the best time to schedule your complimentary needs assessment?

WHAT YOU NEED TO KNOW FROM A CLIENT

Have your questions in front of you. You need as much of a visual of their need as you can obtain from them before you decide you even want to work with them. At a minimum, ask these questions:

- What is the situation from their perspective?

- Is the organizing for the person contacting you, or someone else?

- Do they want hands-on help or advice?

- Is the problem in one room of the house or the entire house? (Or building, office, etc.)

- What is their time frame for getting the job done?

- When can they start?

- Do they have an organizing budget?

- What pets do they have?

- Ask for directions to their location. Don't rely on a web-based mapping tool; they are not always reliable.

- Ask for their home/business/mobile phone numbers.

- Ask for their e-mail address.

YOU HAVE A CONSULTATION SCHEDULED—WHAT'S NEXT?

- Schedule your consultation for no more than an hour if you are not charging for it.

- Record the consultation (time/date and client information) in your time management tool.

- Enter the client information in your contacts database.

- Prepare and take with you a client file including:

  · Map (directions) to client.

  · Client Needs Assessment Questionnaire.

  · Organizing Plan of Action template.

  · Letter of Agreement (the letter of agreement along with a confirmation of your initial session can be sent via e-mail prior to your session).

  · Invoice for needs assessment (if charging).

- Take your camera and tape measure.

CHECKLISTS

See the Forms and Tools section for the checklists and client intake form to use during each of the five phases of the client process to help you be prepared.

✍ EXERCISES

❦ Write your thirty-second hook.

Chapter 11

How to Effectively Conduct a Needs Assessment and Create an Organizing Plan of Action

Description: The needs assessment discoveries will be your road map to clearly identifying your client's goals, needs, barriers, and expectations. This chapter will provide you with questions to ask your client that will help you best assess their organizing needs and from there, develop an organizing plan of action.

- How to conduct an assessment without giving away too much information
- Environmental issues needs assessment questions
- Emotional issues needs assessment questions
- Expectation needs assessment questions
- Creating an organizing plan of action

OVERVIEW

The needs assessment is a tool and process for you to gather information about what the client needs and how you can help them (or not). It can be conducted on the phone, in e-mail form, completing an online form, or in person.

If you are conducting the needs assessment in person and *not charging* for it, you don't want to tell the potential client "how" you are going to help them. Otherwise, they will take all of your useful information and decide to try to do it themselves. Your time is valuable, so limit your in-person needs assessment to less than an hour if you are not charging for it.

If you are charging for the needs assessment, you can promote it as an "Organizing Plan of Action," where you meet with the client in their environment and conduct the needs assessment, but also provide a few ideas that you will incorporate into an overall Organizing Plan of Action that they can then implement on their own, you can work with them to implement, or you can implement the plan for them. This approach can be done by charging for a one hour in-person assessment followed by charging a minimum one-hour of plan development.

If the client has not been disorganized their entire adult life, then usually something happened that caused a change in their life, and their organization systems stopped functioning. This is called "situational disorganization." Some possible causes of situational disorganization are:

- Someone was born or someone died.

- They moved or changed jobs.

- The children moved out or back in.

- They are marrying or divorcing.

- Their hobbies are taking over—the worst are sewing, quilting, or scrapbooking.

- They are creating a home-based business.

- They are selling or buying a home.

- They are downsizing.

- There is a medical condition or aging issues.

Once you are in the door, take a tour of the environment and listen to what the client is saying, but observe everything. Listen for how they speak. Do they sound sad, happy, angry, confused, overwhelmed, or frustrated?

Ask your client the following questions and those found on the Needs Assessment Forms (residential or business) located in the Forms and Tools section, or observe the environment for your answers to these questions.

Environmental Questions
1. What specifically is not working for you?

2. Are you organizing their paper, space, or time?

3. What is working?

4. What is the function of each room and/or how would you like each space to function? (List each room they want you to work in.)

5. Is there too much stuff or not enough storage? Or, a combination of both?

6. Which family members will be working with us and is everyone agreeable to go through this process?

7. Do you prefer things to be out in view or put away out of sight?

8. What is your vision for this space?

9. What are your goals for this space?

Emotional Questions

1. Why do you want to get organized?

   Responses you might hear include:
   - I'm tired of living this way.

   - I can't find what I need when I need it.

   - I want to be a good role model to my children.

   - I want to be more successful in my job.

   - I'm embarrassed to have friends over.

   - I'm feeling out of control.

   - I don't want to continue spending money on items I already have but can't find.

2. What do you think are your barriers?

   Responses you might hear include:
   - My husband/wife is a slob.

   - My children expect me to pick up after them all the time.

   - I'm too busy with my job to keep the house organized.

   - I don't feel well.

   - I'm really tired all the time.

   - There is no place to put anything, nothing makes sense to me.

3. What are you willing to part with? Why or why not?

    Responses you might hear include:
    *   Nothing, I need it all.

    *   It was my mother's/father's and is very sentimental.

    *   I can't get rid of these papers; I might need them someday.

    *   I have gained/lost weight, and I need several sizes of clothes just in case.

    *   I love my books and do not want to sell them.

4. If I could ask you to fill in the remainder of these phrases, what would you say?

    *   I can never find _____.

    *   I don't know what do with _____.

    *   When I try to get organized, I struggle with _____.

    *   What irritates me the most is _____.

    *   What consumes most of my time is _____.

    *   I feel I never get a chance to _____.

    *   It feels like all I ever work on is _____.

    *   I'm really concerned about _____.

History of Disorganization

(a yes answer to all three indicates the person is chronically disorganized).

1. Have you been disorganized most of your adult life?

2. Does your disorganization affect you every day of your life?

3. Have you tried to get organized before?

Expectations

1. What will organized look and feel like to you?

2. What are your expectations of a professional organizer?

3. Do you plan to work with me hands-on or do you prefer to have me work alone and ask you questions as I need to?

4. What must happen for this to be a successful experience for you?

The needs assessment discoveries will be your road map to clearly identifying your client's goals, needs, barriers, and expectations.

Now that you have completed your needs assessment, you have a much better idea of how you are going to help your client. One way to communicate how you are going to help is with an Organizing Plan of Action. See the Forms and Tools section for the Needs Assessment Questionnaires and Organizing Plan of Action template.

An Organizing Plan of Action may include:

- Project timeline.

- Budget.

- Summary of each room's purpose(s).

- Client's goals.

- Client's vision.

- Assignments and procedures.

- Where to place items.

- How and where to contain items.

- Resources including how to repurpose existing materials and additional materials needed.

- Vendors and cost estimate for materials.

- How and where to dispose of items.

- Maintenance plan.

The following is an example of a completed Organizing Plan of Action.

ORGANIZING PLAN OF ACTION—EXAMPLE

Date

Client Name
Street Address
City, State, Zip

Re:

Dear Client,

I enjoyed talking with you about your home organizing needs and goals. I congratulate you on taking that first step toward living your life more purposefully and taking control of your surroundings!

Based on the information gathered during our initial consultation, the enclosed plan covers what we identified as your organizing goals and vision for your office/meditation room.

If you have any questions about any assignment or product I have listed, please contact me for further direction. Please call me if you want me to work with you on implementing your plan and to arrange dates and time to begin.

All the best,

Your name
Your title

Office/Meditation Room

Step 1—Strategize

Vision: An organized work space. A calm, peaceful, and inviting space to meditate.

Current State:

Purposes:

- A place to process incoming and outgoing paper information for the household.

- A place to store paper information.

- A place to meditate.

- A safe place to store family photographs until they can be organized.

- A place to store craft materials.

Goals:

1. Clear the clutter!
2. Make the spaces visually appealing, inviting, and functional.

Step 2—Prioritize, Group, and Reduce

Assignments:

1. Remove built-in shelving.
2. Commit a day to emptying the area of its contents, clean, and evaluate the space.
3. Move items from other areas to the space you are organizing that also need to be part of the grouping and reducing process.
4. Group all like items together by zones (meditation, office, paper, crafts, family archives).
5. Use boxes with labels "keep" (meditation, office, paper, crafts, family archives), "move to another space," "donate," "trash," or "recycle" to sort the items into.
6. Reduce and let go of (donate, sell, trash) anything that you will not use again because of the following criteria:
    a. You don't like it.
    b. You don't need it in your life today.
    c. It's broken, torn, stained—needs repair that you don't have time for or ability.
    d. You haven't used in over six months (other than memorabilia).
    e. It's a duplicate and you only *need* one.
    f. See attached list of donation resources for where to give your discards a new home.

7. Move to the appropriate room anything that doesn't pertain to the function and purposes of this space.

    a. Move Christmas decorations to basement.

    b. Move books to art studio.

    c. Move vacuum cleaner.

Step 3—Localize and Assign a Zone

1. Purpose the space by creating a specific zone for each activity (see floor plan).

    a. Meditation zone

    b. Office zone

    c. Family archive storage zone

    d. Craft materials storage zone

2. Place only the items needed to support each activity in their appropriate zone in containers that are suitable to the item and space.

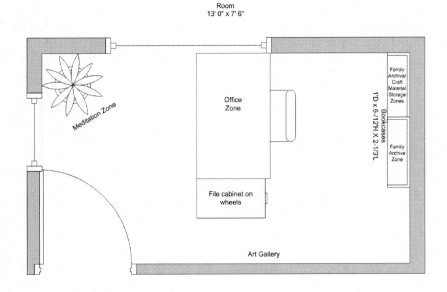

Step 4 —Containerize, Contain, and Label

1. Select containers (see Materials and Resources below for recommendations).
2. Repurpose existing archive storage boxes.
3. Adjust bookcase shelving to the height of storage boxes to maximize space.
4. Install items in containers and label.

Materials to be Repurposed:

- Desk 30"Hx48"Lx30"D (68 "L with drop-leaf extension)

- 2 bookcases 6 ½'Hx28"Lx12"D

- 2 archive storage boxes 10"Hx15"Lx12"D (tan and green)

- 3 archive storage boxes 4"Hx17" Lx12" D (2 green/1tan)

- 1 archive storage boxes 8" Hx12 ½" Lx10 ½"D (charcoal)

- 2 wire photo containers 6"Hx7 ½"Lx15 ½"D

Materials and Resources

Item	Purpose	Suggested Supplier	Estimated Cost
Element File Cabinet on Wheels Natural 15"Wx17"Dx 27"H	Store household files	Storables	$149

Archive Storage Boxes	Store family memorabilia	Container Store	$15–$18 each
Archival Storage Box Letter / Legal Size	Store large photos and papers	Container Store	$17 each
Archival Photo Storage Box	Store photos up to 5"x7"		

Expedit Cube Bookcase	Option for containing craft and family memorabilia	Ikea	$79 each

Step 5— Maximize, Evaluate, and Maintain

1. Is everything as easy as you like it to be?
2. Is the space as you envisioned it in Step 1?
3. Do the zones and categories work well for you?
4. Write a maintenance plan.
5. Follow the maintenance plan for three weeks, and evaluate where it needs to be adjusted.

Donation Drop-Off Locations

What	Who	Phone	Address or Web Site
Books, CDs, DVDs	Public libraries		www.publiclibraries.com
Cellular phones—any	Verizon	1-800-426-2790	www.verizonwireless.com
Clothing	Junior League of Portland	503-297-6364	www.juniorleagueofportland.com
Clothing, Bedding	West Woman's & Children's Shelter	503-224-7718	NW 20th & Kearney, Portland, OR
Computer Equipment	Computer Drive Connection	503 -992-0177	923 N. Fremont Lane, Cornelius
Craft Supplies	SCRAP	503-294-0769	www.scrapaction.org
Debris	Metro Recycling	503-234-3000	www.metro-region.org
Electronic Equipment	Earth Protection Services	503-620-2466	7272 SW Durham Rd, Tigard, OR
Household items	Goodwill		www.locator.goodwill.org
Musical Instruments	Ethos	503-283-8467	www.ethos-inc.org

What	Who	Phone	Address or Web Site
Old House Parts	The Rebuilding Center	503-331-1877	www.rebuildingcenter.org
Wedding Dresses	Making Memories	503-829-4486	www.makingmemories.org
Women's Clothing	Dress for Success	503-249-7300	www.dressforsuccess.org
Women's Clothing	Shepherds Door	503-256-2353	www.portlandrescuemission.org

Donation Pickup Service

What	Who	Phone	Address or Web Site
Household Items	A.R.C.	503-777-4736	www.arcoregon.org
Household Items	OR Community Warehouse	503-235-8786	
Household Items	Salvation Army	503-235-4192	www.tsacascade.org
Household Items	St. Vincent DePaul	503-234-0594	www.svdppdx.org

Other Service Providers

What	Who	Phone	Address or Web Site
Household Items	Dough Nation Services LLC	503-320-8213	www.doughnationservices.com
Household Items	1-800-GOT-JUNK?	503-292-5399	www.1800gotjunk.com

Chapter 12

Scheduling the Job with Your Client

Description: This chapter will explain the components of a Job Agreement and provide you with a template that you can tailor to meet your business needs including:

- Services to be performed
- Fees associated with services
- Time to perform services
- Payment policy
- Cancellation policy
- Materials
- Travel
- Product procurement
- Limitations of liability
- What you will not provide

Disclaimer: I am not engaged in rendering legal advice or services. Therefore, I highly recommend you work with an attorney to prepare your Job Agreement as it will need to be defensible in the state(s) you do business in and by your attorney.

JOB AGREEMENT COMPONENTS (SEE THE FORMS AND TOOLS SECTION FOR AN EXAMPLE OF A SERVICES AND FEES LETTER OF AGREEMENT)

- Services to Be Performed: Clearly state what the client can expect from you for each type of service (needs assessment, consultation, hands-on, coaching, maintenance, etc.)

- Time to Perform Services: Clearly state the minimum and/or maximum amount of time for each type of service (needs assessment, consultation, hands-on, coaching, maintenance, etc.)

What to Say When Asked How Long Implementation Will Take

- Turn the question around and ask the client how long they think it would take them to complete the project on their own?

- Ask, "Do you have a budget for this project?"

- It's a good idea to know what your client is willing to spend to achieve her goals. If it is less than you think you can work with her to complete the project, you can suggest working "hands-on" with her for "X" number of hours and then give her assignments to complete the project. Allow for the expense of consultations and follow-up in between assignments.

- Every client and every situation is unique and cannot be compared. Some factors involved in how long it will take are:

- How difficult it is for the client to make decisions

- How clearly defined the client's goals are

- Say, "Let's work together for X hours and that will give me an idea of how we work together and move through the process."

- Remind them they didn't get disorganized overnight. It will take time to get organized and create new habits and behaviors.

- A range of time based on previous experience.

What Not To Say When Asked How Long
Implementation Will Take

- It is not recommended to quote a specific amount of time it will take to complete a project—unless you are very confident in your quote and you are willing to work for less money if it takes more time than you quoted.

- You will be able to better quote your time after you have worked with a client for two to four hours. You will then know how easy or difficult it is for your client to make decisions.

Julie Morgenstern, in her book *Organizing from the Inside Out,* suggests the following time allotments for each step in different areas of a home:

Area	Sort Purge	Assign a Zone	Contain & Label	Equalize
Attic	16 hours 3 hours	2 hours	3 hours	5 min daily
Basement	16 hours 3 hours	2 hours	3 hours	5 min daily
Bathroom	3 hours 30 min	15 min	3 hours	5 min daily
Bedrooms	4 hours 1 hour	1 hour	3 hours	10 min daily
Closets	3 hours 1 hour	30 min	3 hours	5 min daily
Garage	16 hours 3 hours	2 hours	3 hours	5 min daily
Home Office	16 hours 3 hours	1 hour	6 hours	15 min daily
Household Hubs	4 hours 4 hours	2 hours	6 hours	15 min daily
Kids' Rooms	12 hours 2 hours	1 hour	4 hours	5 min daily
Kitchens	6 hours 2 hours	1 hour	2 hours	15 min daily
Living Room	5 hours 1 hour	30 min	3 hours	5 min daily

- Fees Associated with Services: Clearly state what your fee is for each type of service (needs assessment, consultation, hands-on, coaching, maintenance, etc.)

  · State your fees are exclusive of materials and tools.

  · State your fee for travel, if you have one.

- Payment Policy: Clearly state when payment is due for each service (needs assessment, consultation, hands-on, coaching, maintenance, etc.) From my personal experience, I suggest you get paid at the conclusion of each session, if not before. You could ask for 50 percent deposit. The deposit will commit your client to the session and will give you assurance of payment.

- Cancellation Policy: Forty-eight-hour cancellation policy is standard. You need sufficient time to book a cancellation to recoup your billable hours. Be strict and enforce this policy.

- Limitation of Liability Example: Client will review all materials XYZ Organizing Company recommends to be disposed of by means of recycling, shredding, donation, resale, or any other means agreed to between Client and XYZ Organizing Company Client agrees that XYZ Organizing Company and its employees are not responsible for any loss of damage caused by Client's failure to carefully review or inspect any disposed items. Client also agrees that XYZ Organizing Company and its employees are not liable for any loss or damage, including consequential damages, Client sustains as the result of services or advice provided to Client by XYZ Organizing Company, or its employees, under this Agreement, including any loss or damage caused by the negligence or fault of XYZ Organizing Company or its employees.

- What Is Not Included in Your Services Example: XYZ Company consultants do not provide housecleaning, assembly of furniture, shelving, closet systems, moving of heavy furniture, climbing extension ladders, or any similar type of activities.

- Miscellany Example: This letter of agreement constitutes the understanding of standard XYZ Organizing Company services and fees between the parties. Its terms can be modified only by a written amendment to this agreement, signed by both parties.

- Photographs

  · May we print your before and after pictures for reference materials? **Yes/No**
  · May we include your before and after pictures on our Web site? **Yes/No**
  · If yes, may we list your name or do you prefer anonymity? **List/Anonymity**

- Client signature / date:

- Company signature / date:

OTHER BUSINESS POLICIES TO CONSIDER AND COMMUNICATE

- What are your fees for:

  · Overtime?
  · Leaving early because the client asks to end the session?
  · Client tardiness?

- How are you going to handle:

  · Post-dated checks?
  · Bounced checks?

- Are you going to accept a job out of your normal skill range, for example installing closets or shelving?

- Role boundaries—are you going to:
  - Baby-sit?
  - Run errands?
  - Care for pets?
  - Perform housekeeping services?
  - Care for elders?
- You need to understand and consider the legal or liability issues with caring for children, pets, and elders.

- Communicate and know your region's regulations on transporting hazardous waste and whether or not you will provide that service.

- Are you going to provide the service of dropping off discards (trash) and donations?

- What is your policy on discussing the following subjects about either you or your client:
  - Family members?
  - Sexual preference?
  - Marital status?
  - Religious or spiritual preference?
  - Political affiliations?
  - Physical or mental health?

See the Forms and Tools section for a sample Services and Fees Agreement.

📄 ACTIONS

☐ Draft your Services and Fees Agreement.

☐ E-mail your draft to your attorney for review and input.

☐ Write your business policies.

Chapter 13

5 Steps to Organizing® Process

Description: The 5 Steps to Organizing® process was created in an effort to clearly communicate a consistent methodology of organizing and to transfer organizing skills to my clients. It is a time-tested process that will not only give you a methodology for organizing your clients but, will also teach them the skills they need to maintain their organization and systems after you leave. This chapter covers:

- 5 Steps to Organizing® process details

- Keep–let go criteria for client

- Stumbling block excuses

- Ten organizing principles to maintain organization

Note: The 5 Steps to Organizing® process was created by the author and is a registered trademark of SolutionsForYou, Inc.

5 STEPS TO ORGANIZING®

My 5 Steps to Organizing® process and principles are based on creating new *habits* and behaviors rather than a one-time clean sweep event. The change needs to occur *internally* as well as externally for it to be lasting. Identifying your client's current habits is essential to creating new habits and behaviors toward organization.

The Five Steps to Organizing® are intended to be basic and simple. If a process is too complicated, your client will not be able to follow it or learn basic, but essential, organizing skills.

Step 1— Strategize

Make a plan for your home. This is the first step in the organizing process. Use a spiral notebook to capture thoughts, ideas, and solutions for each room in your home. Assess the causes of disorder so that lasting change can be achieved.

Walk through your home to discover how one room affects another. Rooms in a home must work together in order for an organizing system to be effective and to create flow. Some questions to ask:

- What do you *call* this space?

- What is the *purpose* of this space?

- What *activities* will take place in this space?

- What are your current *habits* with this space?

- Do you have all of the items you need to support those activities?

- What is your *vision* for how the space will look, feel, and function?

Step 2—Prioritize

Realize that organizing is not an overnight process. In this step you are *deciding* what is important to you today.

- Commit a day to emptying the room of its contents, clean, and evaluate the space.

- As you empty the space, place like items together (grouping).

- You will need boxes or designated spaces for: keep, donate, shred, trash, sell, and move.

- Relocate (place in a box labeled "move") or let go of ("donate," "sell," "trash") anything that doesn't pertain to the room's function, activities, and purpose.

- With what is left, reduce (prioritize) and let go of ("donate," "sell," "trash") what doesn't serve a purpose in your life today.

You may have difficulty, or work with someone who has difficulty, letting go of certain items. Questions to help aid you through the decision making process are listed below and can help to clarify what is important and what is no longer important to you (prioritize). Following the keep–let go criteria questions are stumbling block excuses we make for not letting go of an item and responses to help you see a more realistic perspective.

KEEP–LET GO CRITERIA

Practical Questions

1. Is it useful and beautiful to you?

2. Is it a duplicate?

3. Is this the best place for it?

4. If you keep it, will you remember you have it?

5. If you remember you have it, will you be able to find it?

6. How are you going to display it/ store it/use it?

7. Do you have room for it?

8. Do you need it or just want it or neither?

9. How long do you need to keep it? When can you let go of it?

10. Is it too worn/broken/unidentifiable?

11. Is the information still current?

12. Will you actually use it/refer to it?

13. When's the last time you used this item?

14. When do you think you will use it again (or for the first time) and what circumstances will have to be in place in order for you to use it?

15. Is this adding value to your life (or home or business) right now?

16. Can it easily be duplicated or created if needed again?

17. What's the worst that can happen if you toss it?

18. Will you really read it? When?

19. Are you really going to finish this quilt (or other project)? When?

For Clothes

20. Do you feel great in it?

21. Does it match anything?

22. Does it fit well?

23. How many do you have of this? (i.e., how many white T-shirts do you have?)

24. Is this of high value or importance, or is it getting in the way of your ability to find what you need, when you need it?

Emotional Questions

25. Does it make you happy to see it?

26. Does it make you mad, sad, or feel bad to see it?

27. Does it make others unhappy to see it?

28. Do you love it?

29. Are you honoring and enjoying it?

30. Does it lift your spirits to look at it?

31. Where did it come from/who gave it to you? (Sometimes it turns out to have been a gift from someone they left behind long ago, or just don't like.)

32. Are you keeping it because someone gave it to you and you will feel guilty if you get rid of it?

33. If we took a picture of it, would that make it easier for you to let it go?

34. If you knew (or visualized) that someone else would really benefit from having this (i.e., if we found a great place to donate it?), would that make it easier for you to let it go?

35. Convince me that you need to keep it.

When Dealing with Memorabilia

36. Do you have anything else that reminds you of this (event, person, time)?

37. Are you putting things before people and relationships?

Financial/Legal Questions

38. Does it belong to you?

39. Are you legally required to keep it?

40. Would you need this check/document in a legal dispute (i.e., divorce, child custody)?

41. Is there a tax reason to keep it?

42. Will this help you make money?

43. Will this save you money?

44. Would you buy it again?

45. Can you borrow or purchase another one if needed?

46. Does it take more time and effort to manage than it is worth?

47. If you were moving, would you want to pay to have it packed and moved?

48. What does it cost you to keep, store, and maintain it?

49. If you donate it, can you get a deduction?

50. If you sell it, what could you do with the money?

STUMBLING BLOCK EXCUSES

Excuse #1: "I might need it someday."

Look at each item as though you were packing it (or not) for a move. Does the item still have a purpose in your life today? Ask yourself, "If I were to move this item, where would it live in my home?" Why isn't it living there in your current home?

When I hear my client say they might need it someday. I hold up a calendar and say, "I see Sunday, Monday, Tuesday, Wednesday, Thursday, Friday, and Saturday on this calendar—can you show me someday?" I ask them to physically circle a day on the calendar as someday and if they haven't used any of the items they designate as "someday" by that date, they need to donate them. Hanging on to stuff you aren't currently using makes it harder to access the things you are using.

Excuse #2: "I don't know what to keep."

This usually relates to paper. The amount of paperwork you receive can cause you to freeze, especially when much of the paperwork seems to be "important." The U.S. Postal Service attests to the fact that contemporary Americans get more mail in one month than their parents did in an entire year, and more mail in one year than their grandparents received in a lifetime. And, that doesn't include e-mail! It's no wonder we have difficulty discerning what is important.

Essentially, you need to keep paperwork for which you have a purpose. There are five purposes to keep papers: (1) taxes, (2) resale of property/cost basis, (3) agreements you have, (4) certificates/legal proof, and (5) returns (receipts) or disputes (claims). Be clear what that *purpose* is and store the paper so that you can access it when that time comes. Most paper (in fact 80 percent) has no future—toss it!

Excuse #3: "It was a gift."

Once a gift is given to you, you are free to do with it what you choose. The object isn't the gift. The gift is the act— someone thought of you and wanted to express their thoughts in a tangible object. My mom told me when I was child, "It's the thought that counts." Think good thoughts. Now get rid of all those gifts you don't use or love. I'm sure you never gave anyone a gift and thought, "I love you very much, and I hope this is a burden to you for the rest of your life!" The love is in the giving. Use it, love it, or give it to someone who can. You have my permission to get rid of any gift you don't use or love.

Excuse #4: "It reminds me of my mother."

People associate an object with a special memory. The object is not the memory—the memory is inside you. Take a picture and let go of the object. To preserve the memory, write about the memory in a journal and place the picture of the item with your journal entry. There it will be preserved so that you won't forget and generations after you will have the memory too.

Excuse #5: "I paid a lot of money for it."

The monetary value of any item is only that for which you could sell it. Don't hesitate to part with something simply because you paid a lot of money for it. Keeping items that don't serve a purpose in your life today cost you in terms of lost productivity and sacrifice of freedom. Plus it is negative energy. It makes you *mad* that you spent a lot of money for something that you are not using any more and keeping that item around is a constant reminder of that feeling. For example, many people are transitioning from the big, bulky computer monitor or TV and replacing it with a sleek, slim, and sexy flat-screen monitor. Yet, they keep around those big hulky monitors because they paid a lot of money for them. One of the criteria I use with clients in helping them to decide whether or not keep something is that if it makes you feel bad or mad, get rid of it! If you are storing items in an offsite storage unit consider the cost savings you will have if you no longer need the storage unit.

Excuse #6: "I don't have the time to get organized!"

I would be a very wealthy person if I had fifty dollars for every time I hear this excuse! Granted our "free time" is very precious, and the last thing you want to do is spend your limited free time eliminating the clutter in your life.

But, clutter monopolizes our time. How much time do you spend looking for your keys, an unpaid bill, or the permission slip for your kid's field trip? Does watching a favorite DVD involve sorting through your disorganized collection—so you go out and rent a movie you already own? The time you lose because of the clutter is easily doubled when you consider the time, energy, and effort that are sapped from you mentally and psychologically. One effect of clutter is that you shut down. You have to spend all your energy just coping with the mess, rather than tending to the things that really matter to you. No matter how deep the clutter is, you can make the time to free yourself from it. It's an investment in yourself that will turn things around. And, after you've made that investment and created new habits with your new systems, the time spent will come back to you with compounded interest!

Step 3—Localize

Assign a specific purpose for each room in your home. This may sound simple, but things become nomadic when there is not a predetermined place to store them. Knowing the function (purpose) of each room in your home eliminates the constant decision making process of putting things away.

- Evaluate the desired activities for each room in your home and plan to store the items that support those activities nearby.

- Create specific zones in each room for each activity.

- Place only the items needed to support each activity in their appropriate zone.

- Place the items you need to access frequently in "prime real estate" spaces and items you don't need to access frequently in the other spaces.

Step 4—Containerize

- What items need containers?

- Measure items to be contained.

- Determine number of containers based on volume.

- Decide on container material (wood, metal, plastic, woven).

- Label the containers.

Step 5—Maximize

Organization is an ongoing process. As our lives change, so do our organizing needs. It is imperative to reassess the rooms in your home on a regular basis and make changes when necessary.

Organization is not neatness. In my experience, stress does not come from clutter. It comes from not knowing where to put the clutter away. My home gets messy as my family and I go about living. The difference that organizing makes is that I know where to put the mess away and can have it cleaned up in a short amount of time, without resorting to the shove and close method. That gives me peace of mind.

Ask your client these questions:

- Is the space now as you envisioned in Step 1?

- What new habits do you need to create?

- Are the systems working?

- Can you maintain it on a regular basis?

- What will that maintenance plan be?

165

A maintenance plan addresses what needs to be done and at what frequency, such as daily, weekly, monthly, etc. as illustrated in this example for maintaining a kitchen pantry:

- Daily keep the zones intact.

- Weekly replenish your pantry with items that have been used.

- Monthly toss expired/stale food items.

- Semiannually reevaluate your zones and adjust accordingly.

TEN ORGANIZING PRINCIPLES

The following organizing principles are beneficial in maintaining organization and can be incorporated into a client's maintenance plan where suitable:

1. One in–one out: When something new comes into your home, something must leave.

2. Before you buy: Before you buy an item, decide where it will "live" in your home. If you don't know, don't buy. Go home, look around, and if you can find a place for the item, then you buy it, otherwise you pass on the purchase. Also, consider if you really need the item.

3. Containers: Buy containers only when you know what will go in them. Containers are often purchased to "solve an organizing problem" only to create more clutter because the owner doesn't know what to do with them or where to place them.

4. Label: Label shelves, containers, drawers, etc. So you know where to put away something, and more importantly so that others you share your home with know where to put away something. A label can be words, pictures, or a combination of both.

5. Don't zigzag: Choose an area to organize and stick with that area. If you find something that belongs in another area of your home, don't move it until you are finished organizing the space you started in. Otherwise you spend too much time moving from room to room relocating stuff and you lose focus on your original task. Place items to move to another area in a box marked "move." When you are finished with your task, then you can walk around your home and put away the stuff in the "move box."

6. Prioritize: Keeping everything makes nothing important. Decide what is truly important in your life and that will help you focus on what to keep and honor.

7. Be decisive: Clutter is caused by deferred decisions. Don't wait to make a decision about where something belongs; decide immediately and put it there. Return it to its "home" whenever it wanders away.

8. Set a limit: Set a limit on how many of something you are going to keep. For example, magazines. Decide to keep one year's worth of each subscription that you will refer to and recycle the rest. Another example is to set a limit on the amount of space you are allocating to a collection.

167

9. Paper: Ask yourself, "Can I get this information somewhere else, such as the Internet or the library?" If you can easily access the information somewhere else, you don't need to keep the piece of paper—toss it! Only 20 percent of what you file for reference you will actually refer to. File wisely!

10. Maintenance: Organizing is not a one-time "clean sweep" event. Create and follow a maintenance plan for all the areas in your life and home. You can do all the grouping, reducing, and organizing you want, but if you don't learn the skills and follow a plan you will backslide.

✍ EXERCISES

> ⚑ Practice the 5 Steps to Organizing ® process in your
> environment, with a family member, or friend.

Chapter 14

Client Follow-Up aka Preventative Backsliding

Description: Recognize backsliding and effective ways to address it with a client with these follow-up practices:

- Thank-you note
- Follow-up appointment
- Evaluation
- Client Satisfaction Survey

THANK-YOU NOTE

- Send immediately after implementation is completed.

- Do you want your client to remember you long after you have left? Send a thank-you note *immediately* after your final implementation appointment.

- Do you want to make a lasting impression? Send a handwritten thank-you note.

- Be sure to enclose your business card and before/after pictures!

FOLLOW-UP APPOINTMENT

- The purpose of a follow-up appointment is to make sure the systems and solutions you and your client implemented are working for her.

- A client will backslide within thirty days of implementation.

- Schedule a follow-up appointment within thirty days at the conclusion of the final implementation appointment.

Evaluation

- Is everything working the way the client envisioned?

- Have the goals of the client been met?

- Is your client able to follow the maintenance plan?

CLIENT SATISFACTION SURVEY

The purpose of a client satisfaction survey is to provide you, the professional organizer, with feedback on your services and meeting the client's expectations. You can include the survey in your thank-you note or as a follow-up e-mail. You could also create the survey with an online tool, such as surveymonkey.com, to collect and analyze your client feedback. Some questions to ask are:

1. Did XYZ Organizing Company provide you with confidential and empathetic advice? If not, please explain.

2. Did XYZ Organizing Company provide you with ideas

and solutions, along with hands-on help in organizing chaotic areas? If not, please explain.

3. What ideas or solutions helped you to get organized the most?

4. Do you feel you will be able to maintain the organizing systems XYZ Organizing Company helped you to establish? If not, please explain.

5. Did XYZ Organizing Company meet your expectations? If not, please explain.

6. Did XYZ Organizing Company work within your desired timeline? If not, please explain.

7. Please write a brief client appraisal statement for our records. May we print this statement on our reference listing and on our Web site? **Yes/No**

8. If yes, may we list your name or do you prefer anonymity?

9. Please provide any other comments and suggestions you have for us.

10. Would you be willing to be a reference for XYZ Organizing Company?

11. Would you recommend XYZ Organizing Company to others? If not, please explain.

12. Do you know of others who could benefit from XYZ Organizing Company services? If yes, please provide their name and phone number below.

📄 ACTIONS

☐ Create your client satisfaction survey. An online tool you can create your client satisfaction survey with is www.surveymonkey.com.

Chapter 15

Working with Clients on Paper Management

Description: This chapter will teach you techniques and systems for how to work with clients on organizing their household paper information including:

- Benefits of organizing your paper information

- The A.R.T. of paper management

- How to create a paper processing center

- Where to start

- File strategies

- How to identify what paper to toss and what to keep (and for how long)

- Where and how to keep your paper information

- Products and systems that can help you organize paper information

- Products that can help track finances

Note: The content of this chapter is written for you to communicate to your clients, rather than to you the professional organizer. However, the information may also be of value to you in organizing your own paper documents. The information may be reproduced by you, the professional organizer, to present at workshops.

BENEFITS OF ORGANIZING YOUR PAPER INFORMATION

A benefit of organizing your paper is you will know where to look for the information you need for many transactions such as:

- Financial and estate planning

- Investment options

- Refinancing

- Bill Paying

- Tax Preparation

- Health Records

- Educational Records

- Loans

When your paper is processed, acted on, and stored properly you are rewarded with the benefits of effective record keeping. You will be able to find the information you need, when you need it. The result is a less cluttered environment and mind allowing you to focus on your priorities and goals and not piles of paper.

THE A.R.T OF PAPER MANAGEMENT

Information comes to us in many forms, but most predominately in paper form. It arrives from snail mail, e-mail, children's backpacks, spouse's briefcases, and many other avenues. We know how we obtain paper information, it's what we do with it after it arrives that many struggle with. The following Paper Information Organizational Chart will help you to picture how to process your paper information so that it goes where it belongs. A matching system should be created for your electronic information. Sort your paper by:

Action

Reference

Toss

PAPER INFORMATION ORGANIZATIONAL CHART

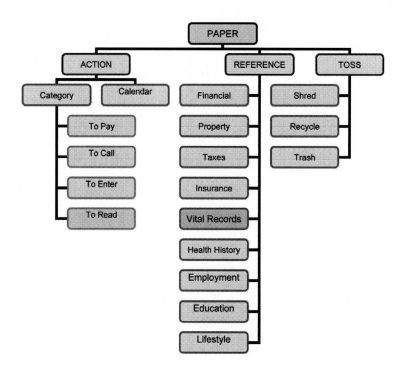

CREATE A PAPER PROCESSING CENTER

Assign an area for each activity within the paper processing center including an area for:

- Action papers

- Reference papers to file

- Trash

- Recycling

- Shredder or container for materials to be shredded

Move items needed to support each paper processing activity to its zone such as containers for trash, recycling, reference papers to file and for action papers, and a shredder. Below is a physical office layout of each paper processing activity zone.

Create a Paper Processing Area

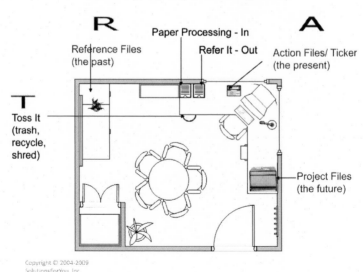

WHERE TO START

Start with the papers that are your most recent (within the past month). Once you have processed your recent papers, you can address your piles of paper and filed papers in old systems.

FILE STRATEGIES

The number one question you will hear from clients is, "How do I decide what paper is important and how long do I keep it?" Before deciding whether or not to keep a piece of paper, you need to decide its purpose. Is it information you will refer to later, or is it something you need to take action on? If it something you will refer to later, do you need to keep the information in paper form or can it be kept electronically? If the paper information is something you are actively working on now it is considered an "action paper." Action papers will usually sit out on a desk or work space for quick and easy access. If the information is something you will need to refer to later, such as last year's income tax records, warranties, or an insurance contract, put it in a "to file" folder or container to be filed in a reference or archive filing system.

WHAT TO KEEP AND HOW LONG

Each situation is unique. For your financial records, always seek the advice of a CPA for your specific requirements. You do need to keep paperwork for which you have a purpose. Five purposes to keep papers are (1) taxes, (2) resale of property/cost basis, (3) agreements you have, (4) certificates/legal proof, and (5) returns (receipts) or disputes (claims). Some questions to ask to help you decide if you need to keep a piece of paper are:

1. Are you legally required to keep it?

2. Would you need this check/document in a legal dispute (i.e., divorce, child custody)?

3. Is there a tax reason to keep it?

4. Is the information still current?

5. Will you actually refer to it later?

6. When's the last time you used this item?

7. Can it easily be duplicated or created if needed again?

8. What's the worst that can happen if you toss it?

9. Will you really read it? When?

How and Where to Keep the Paper Management System

Choose a labeling system for both your action papers and your reference papers that works best for how the person the file system is being created for thinks about accessing this information.

Action Papers

Keep action files in vertical view on the desk top in a file box. Typical actions are:

- To Pay

- To Call

- To Enter

- To Read

Reference Papers

Reference papers belong in a reference filing system in labeled files, by category and alphabetical. Prepackaged file kits can be helpful in determining categories and preparing labels. Such as File Solutions® Home Filing System (www.filesolutions.com), Freedom Filer (www.freedomfiler.com), and Paper Tiger (www.thepapertiger.com). Depending on volume, store the reference documents in a file cabinet or an archive file box. Prepare a hanging file folder tab for each *main category* and manila file folder and label for each *subcategory*. Typical categories or labels for reference/archive papers are:

- Finances (credit card statements, bank statements, utility statements, medical payments)

- Taxes

- Insurance

- Personal property (home records, vehicle records)

- Vital records (passport, birth certificate, etc.)

- Health history

- Employment records

- Education records

- Lifestyle (travel, decorating ideas, pets, recipes, etc.)

PRODUCTS/SYSTEMS FOR YOUR REFERENCE PAPERS— TAX RECORDS

Use one thirteen-pocket accordion file for each tax year and file your paper information in the following categories:

1. Tax filing

2. Financial reports

3. Investment documents

4. Bank statements

5. Credit card year-end summary

6. Income documents

7. Charitable deductions

8. Medical expenses

9. Miscellaneous expenses

10. Child care expenses

11. Business expenses

12. and 13. are empty or for other categories you define

PRODUCTS/SYSTEMS FOR TRACKING YOUR FINANCES

Financial software such as Quicken or QuickBooks to:

- Download and track your checking, savings, and credit card accounts—in one place.

- Create and follow a budget.

- Schedule payments and pay bills right from Quicken.

- Verify accuracy of your bank statements and avoid any inappropriate fees or charges.

- Simplify tax preparation find hidden tax deductions and transfer information directly to TurboTax® software.

PRODUCTS/SYSTEMS FOR DIGITAL FINANCIAL RECORDS

Not all information needs to be kept in paper form. The more paper information you can store in a digital form, the less physical space you will need to store information. One tool that can aid you in storing information digitally is the NeatDesk from www.neatco.com. NeatDesk is a high-speed desktop scanner and digital filing system that scans receipts, business cards, and documents all in one batch. It includes NeatWorks software that identifies and extracts the important information and automatically organizes it for you.

MAINTENANCE—THE KEY

The key to maintaining organized papers is to *regularly* process papers. To maintain your paper, establish and practice the following routines.

Daily: Open mail and sort. Note any action items in your calendar or on your to-do list. Note any events in your calendar. Shred or recycle any unnecessary mail. File any documents that don't require action in your reference file system. File any action papers in your action paper system.

Daily: Review your calendar and update.

Daily: At the end of day, clear your work surface of papers, files, and supplies. Jot down notes with your last thoughts or actions on projects, so you can pick up easily where you left off. Return project and action folders that may have piled up during the day to a vertical system on your work surface if they are still "active." Once "inactive," they should find a place in your reference file system in a file drawer. Put away any materials you've taken out. Returning them to their designated place now will save time when they are needed again.

Daily: Write a to-do list. Make a written plan now for tomorrow. While unfinished tasks, new priorities, and lingering details are still fresh in your mind, write them down. Review your calendar, e-mail messages, and voice mail messages for meetings and appointments that may require prep time. Noting your to-dos on either paper or in an electronic format will keep them handy and easy to find for review and updates the next day. Prioritize your to-dos and schedule them into your calendar *when* you will complete them.

Semimonthly: Pay your bills.

Annually: Purge your file system. A good time to do this is after you have prepared your tax filing.

🗎 ACTIONS

☐ Present a paper management workshop using the material from this chapter.

☐ Review and become familiar with the products mentioned in this chapter (www.filesolutions.com, www.fredomfiler.com, www.thepapertiger.com, www.neatco.com, www.quicken.com, and www.quickbooks.com).

Chapter 16

Working with Clients on Time Management

Description: This chapter covers how to work with clients to manage their time efficiently including:

- Identifying where your time is spent and discover time robbers through a time mapping technique

- What causes procrastination

- Defining your roles and goals for each

- Weekly plan—Learn how to categorize and group activities to effectively manage yourself

- Identify and choose "one" time management system and tool that is right for you and why

Note: The content of this chapter is written for you to communicate to your clients, rather than to you the professional organizer. However, the information may also be of value to you in managing your own time. The information may be reproduced by you, the professional organizer, to present at workshops.

WHERE ARE YOU SPENDING YOUR TIME?

The time map in the Forms and Tools section will give you a clear picture of how you are currently spending your time. It is a great tool to use with clients as well as for your own evaluation. In order to become proactive with your time you need to know where you are spending your time each day. The most effective way to discover how you are spending your time is to complete a Time Map for at least one week.

How to Use the Time Map

Fill in each one-hour block for one week with general *categories* of activities such as personal care, opening mail, attending meetings, interruptions, talking on the phone, computer time, specific work activities, family time, travel time, etc.

The key is to be specific and fill out your Time Map every fifteen minutes or so, noting exactly what just happened. This is similar to a food/exercise log. Document everything you did, including who you talked to and about how long it took. Include:

- Each time you pick up the phone to make or receive a call

- Interruptions and why

- Travel time

- Note how you feel, whether alert, bored, tired, energetic, etc

- Note what your activity *categories* are

- At the end of the week:

- Color each *category* a different color to visually see how much time you are spending in each category.

- Search for patterns not only how you are spending your time, but how your time is spent by others.

- Identify your peak energy times and your low energy times.

What Did You Learn?

- What was your biggest surprise?

- What are you the most proud of?

- What is something you would like to change?

- What was your biggest time waster?

- What is one thing you would like to have more time for?

- What is one thing you want to spend less time on?

- Do your activities support your goals? If not which activities do not?

WHAT CAUSES PROCRASTINATION?

If you don't know why you are delaying doing a certain task, ask yourself this simple question, "Why am I putting it off?" You will most likely answer, "Because I don't want (or don't like) to do it." Fair enough. Now ask yourself, "What is it about the task I don't like or want to do?" It most likely falls into one or more of these six barriers:

1. You consider it a low-priority task (when it is not one).

2. You do not have all the information necessary to make a decision.

3. You have not set aside a specific time to do it.

4. The task seems overwhelming.

5. Something keeps you from achieving the task (often the perfectionist need).

6. You do not know what steps to take to achieve the task.

Once you have identified your roadblocks and the steps you need to take, write down those steps and then schedule them in order.

PLANNING YOUR TIME

Consider what you learned from your Time Map activity as you make a plan for your time. Next ask yourself, "What roles do I play in my life?" For example, my roles are spouse, mother, daughter, sister, business owner, volunteer, friend, and teacher. Using the Weekly Plan handout located in the Forms and Tools section, list your roles horizontally at the top of the plan. Underneath each role, write your goals for the week. Now you can schedule your time as you would like to based upon your priorities. Take some time once a week to plan your week and to evaluate how your schedule is working. Using the Weekly Plan:

- List the tasks associated with each goal. Your tasks can be prioritized with A, B, C, D, or E.

- **A** task that is very important and something *you must* do. You may have more than one "A" task. You can prioritize these by writing "A-1," "A-2," and so on. A-1 is your ugliest task!

- **B** = A task that *you should* do. Reviewing an unimportant phone call or reviewing your e-mail is a B Task.

- **C** = A task that would be *nice* to do, but left undone would not suffer great consequences such as, phoning a friend or having lunch with a co-worker.

- **D** = A task that you can *delegate* to someone else to free up more time for your **A** tasks such as, your teenage child doing his own laundry instead of you doing it.

- **E** = An activity that you can *eliminate* altogether such as watching television.

- Schedule your to-do tasks. The main reason people don't complete their to-do tasks is because they don't plan *when* they will do them.

- Enter your appointments and other commitments in your plan.

- Group like activities together.

- Allow sufficient time for all activities and set limits for each activity.

TIME MANAGEMENT TOOLS

Your specific tool will help you decide how you can:

- Delegate activities to others

- Say *no* to other activities

- Eliminate activities

- Limit yourself to one method if possible and consolidate all calendars into one

- Prioritize what must happen each day...high, medium, or low importance

Choosing the right time management tool for you is critical to managing and planning your time. There are essentially two choices: paper or electronic.

The pros of a paper planning tool are:

- Least expensive

- Easiest

- Simple

- Access anywhere

- Won't crash

- Multiple sizes

- Great overview of schedule (can view month easier than on PDA)

The cons of a paper planning tool are:

- Space can be limiting

- Searching takes longer

- Backup requires copying

- If lost may not have a backup.

- Archival takes up physical space.

- Manually time intensive (rewriting to dos from day to day).

Answer yes or no to each of the following questions. If you answer yes to most of the questions below, a paper planning tool is right for you:

1. I like to see a broad overview of my time, such as a week or month at a glance .**Y / N**

2. I am the only one who needs to see my calendar. **Y / N**
3. I like the feel of pen to paper, textures, colors, and designs of paper. **Y / N**
4. I can remember appointments and tasks when I write them down. **Y / N**
5. I like rewriting my tasks. **Y / N**
6. I like the act of physically checking off or crossing out my completed tasks. **Y / N**
7. Writing helps me think through what I need to do. **Y / N**

The pros of an electronic planning tool are:
- Portable

- Small and hold a lot of information

- Can easily move unfinished tasks from day-to-day without rewriting

- Easy to schedule repetitive meetings, reminders, etc.

- Can set reminder alarms

- Easy to back up

- Can serve as a communication tool (e-mail, Internet, computer files)

The cons of an electronic planning tool are:
- View one screen at a time—limited view of schedule

- It can crash

- Need to keep it charged

- Need to synchronize it with computer to avoid over scheduling

Answer yes or no to each of the following questions. If you answer yes to most of the questions below, an electronic planning tool is right for you:

1. I like the combination calendar, tasks, contacts, and phone all in one. **Y / N**

2. I consider myself a techno-geek, or I like technology and new gadgets. **Y / N**

3. I can remember appointments and tasks when I type or key them. **Y / N**

4. I like knowing my calendar, contacts, and tasks are backed up. **Y / N**

5. I need others to be able to view my calendar and schedule. **Y / N**

6. I like alarm reminders. **Y / N**

7. I like entering a recurring event once and not writing it over and over. **Y / N**

🖹 ACTIONS

☐ Present a time management workshop using the material from this chapter.

☐ Complete the time map exercise for one week.

Chapter 17

Working with Clients on Clutter Control

Description: This chapter covers how to help your clients deal with clutter by asking simple questions about what they really need and about their relationship with clutter. You will learn how to identify what their stumbling blocks are to letting go, how to move through them to achieve a clutter-free space, and how to create a visual plan of what you want your client's space to look and feel like. You will also learn how to teach your clients to stop cluttering and start organizing including:

- What clutter is

- Why clutter happens

- The costs of clutter

- The benefits of eliminating clutter

- Your relationship with clutter

- How to create a visual plan of what you want your space to look and feel like

- How to stop cluttering and start organizing

- The key to staying organized—ten basic organizing principles

Note: The content of this chapter is written for you to communicate to your clients, rather than to you the professional organizer. However, the information may also be of value to you in controlling your own clutter. The information may be reproduced by you, the professional organizer, to present at workshops.

WHAT IS CLUTTER?

Clutter is anything that *is not* serving a purpose in your life *today*. Clutter is things you do not need, use, or love. Clutter is anything that is unfinished. This usually relates to projects that are started and never finished—the memory books and craft projects are typical examples.

WHY DOES CLUTTER HAPPEN?

Clutter is caused by deferred decisions. Clutter and procrastination go hand in hand. Look around at your clutter. Most of it occurs because you haven't taken the time to *decide* where it belongs.

WHAT IS CLUTTER COSTING YOU?

Clutter costs you time, space, money, energy, and relationships. The time it takes you to find what you are looking for because of your clutter. The space you could create for what is truly important to you if it weren't for all of your clutter. The money you spend paying for duplicate items because you can't find what you are looking for—or—didn't remember you already own. The energy you expend investing in taking care of all your clutter. The impact your clutter has on your relationships because others don't want to live with your clutter.

Clutter gets in the way of you pursuing any passion or pleasure because you are too busy taking care of and thinking about your clutter. Clutter weighs you down physically, emotionally, and mentally. You need to free up physical space to open up space [physically and mentally] in your life for new relationships and personal pleasures or pursuits. It comes down to these questions—do you value your stuff over your relationships, your things over your goals, or your possessions over the vision you have for your life?

WHAT ARE THE BENEFITS OF ELIMINATING CLUTTER?

You will regain what your clutter is costing you; time, space, money, energy, and relationships. You will find what you need when you need it. Your self-confidence will increase as you become more organized. You will want people to visit your home again. You will be able to focus on what is important to you instead of on your clutter.

UNDERSTANDING YOUR RELATIONSHIP WITH *YOUR* CLUTTER

Let's take a look at how you relate to your clutter.
Choose from one of the following:

1. Write the story your clutter tells you.

2. Draw the story of your clutter.

3. Take pictures of your clutter.

Next answer these questions:

1. What's working?

2. What's not working?

3. Where are you stuck and why?

4. What is most important for you to accomplish?

Question why and how you accumulate your "stuff":

1. Did you inherit it and feel guilty about letting go of it?

2. Do you go to the mall when you feel depressed?

3. Are you addicted to catalogs or online shopping?

4. Other—how do you collect your "stuff"?

You can choose to stop accumulating more clutter once you understand where it is coming from and why.

HOW TO CREATE A VISUAL PLAN OF WHAT YOU WANT YOUR SPACE TO LOOK AND FEEL LIKE

Now that you have a picture of where you are at, it is time to develop a plan for where you want to go. Choose from the following:

1. Make a list of the areas of clutter that are driving you crazy and schedule when you will address each area on your calendar.

1. _____
2. _____
3. _____
4. _____

2. Draw a picture or create a collage of what you want your space to look like.

3. Describe your top three decluttering priorities.
   1. _____
   2. _____
   3. _____

4. Write your vision of what you want your space to look and feel like.

HOW TO STOP CLUTTERING AND START ORGANIZING

Sometimes just knowing how to *stop* cluttering and where to *start* organizing is the most daunting part of the organizing process. Here are a few rules of thumb to follow when you head down your path to a more organized and clutter-free life:

Begin with Your Biggest Frustration
- Ask yourself what is causing you the most *frequent frustration*—that is where you want to start.

- Is it that pile of paper on top of your kitchen counter?

- Is it your kitchen pantry?

- Is it never finding your keys as you start to head out the door each day?

- Is it your child's, once again, late homework project?

Plan Your Attack
- Plan time for your organizing project. Four-hour blocks work best.

- Have the materials and resources you need on hand (garbage bags, drop box, stickers/labels to identify where items will go, and boxes for sorting).

- Don't buy containers until you have sorted and purged your items to know how many you need.

- Arrange with the charity of your choice to pick up your items for donation immediately after your organizing project is completed.

Work with Others and Systematically
- Working with someone can *help you stay focused* and is more energizing and fun.

- Ask a friend to help you get organized and return the same favor or for another trade.

- You may even consider hiring a professional organizer if you feel you need expert solutions and systems.

- Focus on the task—*don't zigzag*! Start working in one area and stick with it until it is finished.

Look out for the stumbling block excuses and to maintain your newly organized space follow the ten organizing principles, both discussed in Chapter 13.

✎ EXERCISES

✦ Present a clutter control workshop using the material from this chapter.

Chapter 18

The Challenging Clients You Will Meet

Description: Challenging can mean so many things— difficulty focusing, an inability to maintain organizing systems due to chronic disorganization and ADD, students learning organizing skills, seniors and fatigue, and safety issues to consider. This chapter will prepare you for those more challenging clients with an in-depth look at real client case studies.

- Clients with depression

- Clients with attention deficit disorder (ADD)

- Chronically disorganized (CD) clients

- Clients who hoard

- Senior clients

- Student clients

- Safety issues and tactics

CASE STUDIES

As you read about these case studies, think about who is your ideal client. Who do you really want to work with? How does the assessment of your skills connect to these clients? Do you have the skills and knowledge and compassion to help these types of clients? Is this an area you would like to make your specialty? Which characteristics of a professional organizer will help you in working with these types of clients? Which do you possess?

Go back to Chapter 1 and look at those characteristics we discussed that might help you with the clients reviewed in this chapter. Consider your skills and background to evaluate which client base is best for you. You do not have to work with anyone and everyone that comes your way. That is a challenging statement when you are first starting out and you don't have a lot of clients and you want to work. So you think, "Ok I'll try that." But, you need to consider your skills, training, and experience and whether or not you are capable of working with these client types. There is an organization called the National Study Group on Chronic Disorganization and their web site is www.NSGCD.org. You are eligible to become a member after one year as a professional organizer, member of NAPO, or member of Professional Organizers of Canada. They have a tremendous wealth of teleclasses that cover these client types and much more that can provide you with foundational training for working with these clients.

The clients discussed in this chapter may make your heart sing, or they may make you think, "No way!" And, that is OK. Whichever it is, be true to yourself and to your client in working with them; otherwise you are doing both a disservice.

Please realize not all your clients will be like the ones discussed in this chapter. The purpose of this chapter is to make you aware of these client types.

DEPRESSION

The first client I'm going to discuss is my client who has depression. Not only depression, but also attention deficit disorder and is chronically disorganized. What I first noticed in the living room was a roll of paper towels amongst all the clutter. I thought, "Hmm that's odd." But, as I walked through the house, there was a roll in each room. And, as I worked with my client, she would have such an emotional response to the process that she would sob great tears, tears so big that tissues could not absorb them, only paper towels could.

Condition of the Environment

An enormous amount of clutter was present and the environment was not clean. There was evidence of mice droppings. Groceries were left in bags on the floor of the kitchen because there wasn't room in the cabinets to store them.

Techniques Used to Work with the Client

The client and I established clear criteria for what to keep, that I had to continually remind her of and rationalize.

Any Resistance

Huge resistance to letting go of anything—all the way down to her son's baby blanket fuzz balls that she keeps in jars. She continually went dumpster diving after I left each session. This went on for six months, working with her a couple of sessions a week. There was continual back-sliding after each session.

Results

I was able to declutter the living room space, spare bedroom, and son's bedroom. Then she had surgery, and I didn't hear back from her even after leaving a number of messages.

What I Learned

Many of the conditions mentioned before (ADD, CD, depression) were evident together in this client. If someone has ADD, they may also be depressed, which often leads to hoarding. You may need to know if your client is on medication and if it is working. I also learned it is absolutely essential to work in collaboration with the client's therapist. I was able to help her determine criteria for what to let go of and work her through the declutter process. But, the emotional response she had to letting go of her stuff, she needs her therapist to help her with. I am not equipped to provide therapy and should not as a professional organizer. That is not my role, and I am not trained or licensed to do so.

ATTENTION DEFICIT DISORDER

Condition of the Environment

A beautiful home. Clean. Most spaces cluttered. Paper (years of it) was being kept in beautiful baskets and bags. Every time the cleaning crew came to clean the home, all surfaces were swept of paper into these baskets and bags and then forgotten and not dealt with.

This client discovered and communicated to me that she was diagnosed with ADD when her son was diagnosed with ADD. When a child has ADD, one or both of the parents has ADD. She was relieved to find out there was a reason why she is the way she is.

Techniques Used to Work with the Client

We spent several days sorting those years of bags and baskets of paper. Then I set up a file system for her and taught her how to use it.

Once we completed that process, I had gained her trust, and she said to me, "I have a room I would like to show you that I think you can help me with." I said, "Great, where is this room?" She said, "Upstairs. It's the bonus room." Next we spent a week sorting and purging her bonus room. We defined her space as her "creativity center" to give it purpose to help us determine the criteria for what would stay in the creativity center and what didn't belong there.

Any Resistance

This client did not offer much resistance. She was ready to make changes. She wanted to keep more than I recommended—mostly paper. But, overall she was highly motivated to clear out the clutter. Once she was on medication, everything became 3-D where before the clutter was wallpaper to her and she didn't see it.

Results

- She has maintained the space since August 2003.

- She lost fifty pounds.

- She has taught friends how to set up a paper management system.

- She was interviewed in *More Magazine* about the best investment she ever made in her life, which was hiring a professional organizer. A great testament to our industry that someone thought and publically stated that this was the best investment they ever made.

What I Learned

- ADD that is diagnosed in adults can be a relief or a death sentence to your client. For my client, it was a relief, and she was ready to take action and deal with her disorganization.

- Many will be in denial or blame others for their situation.

- They may know that they need your help but are not willing to accept it.

- Other techniques for working with ADD clients:[1]

    · Find out how and where clients work the best. Find a quiet place to work or study. ADD individuals are distracted by sounds that may not distract others.

    · Timers, watches with timers, or an alarm clock help ADD clients stay on schedule. Set time limits to avoid hyperfocusing.

    · Visuals are a must for ADD clients. Calendars, wipe-and-write boards, Post-it® notes, or pictures are a few visuals that create reminders for the client.

    · Encourage your client to delegate the things they don't like doing or are not good at doing. This could be hiring a housekeeper, a coach, an accountant, or an assistant.

    · Emphasize the client work on doing the things they are good at doing.

    · Assist clients in making homes for things where

they use them. This way they won't get distracted looking for lost things.

- Have your client create a home for bills. Devise a bill paying system for them to use.

- If a task is overwhelming, help your client break up the task into smaller parts that are achievable.

- Encourage your client to ask questions out loud. Hearing what one needs to do can move the decision making process along.

- Teach your clients to do one task at a time. Examples of this include collecting trash from all over the house at the same time, and putting all dishes in the dishwasher at one time.

CHRONICALLY DISORGANIZED

Definition of Chronic Disorganization
Chronic disorganization is having a past history of disorganization in which self-help efforts to change have failed, an undermining of current quality of life due to disorganization, and the expectation of future disorganization.[2]

Characteristics of Chronically Disorganized
- Accumulations of large quantities of possessions or paper beyond apparent usefulness or pleasure.

- A high degree of difficulty or discomfort letting go of things.

- A wide range of interests, unfinished projects, and incomplete tasks.

- Reliance on visual cues like paper piles or stacks of things as reminders to take action.

- A tendency to be easily distracted or to lose concentration.

- A tendency to lose track of time.

Condition of the Environment
A beautiful home. Clean, but very cluttered.

Techniques Used to Work with the Client
It was an ongoing process of three-hour sessions every three weeks. Body doubling is the process she responds to. According to Judith Kohlberg,[2]

- A body double is not an active assistant who does not touch anything.

- A body double's principal job is to occupy space while you do organizing chores.

- A body double must be quiet and nondistracting.

- A body double cannot be judgmental.

- A body double must be patient and able to sit still for long periods of time.

After two and a half years she finally allowed me to sort and organize certain areas. Before that, my sole role was to be a body double. We sorted many of her items into boxes that were stored for her to "deal with" when we were "done."

Any Resistance
Tremendous resistance to me touching anything or sorting.

Results

We did get her dining room organized, including a custom-built hutch. We organized her storage rooms after she had an unfortunate sewage backup event that destroyed a lot of what was stored there and she was devastated about that. The bedroom was an ongoing struggle. One day she just stopped responding to my calls and e-mails.

What I Learned

- CD people don't respond well to traditional organizing practices. You will need to be creative with them in your organizing methods. Make it a game of organizing, such as instead of picking out what to toss, pick out what to keep (treasure hunt).[2]

- This category of clients will make you think you are not doing your job well, because every time you go back, you do the same thing all over.

- The client, however, sees tremendous progress after each session.

- Someone is CD are if they answer yes to these three questions:[2]

  1. Have you been disorganized most of your adult life?

  2. Does your disorganization affect you every day of your life?

  3. Have you tried to get organized before?

CLIENTS WHO HOARD

Characteristics of People Who Hoard[3]
According to the Fairfax County Health Department,
Virginia:[3]

- People who hoard are not limited to any age, race,
  gender, or nationality.

- Hoarding behavior can begin early in life but is more
  prevalent in older adults.

- People who hoard can be of any educational or
  socioeconomic level.

- They are unaware that their living circumstances pose
  a danger to themselves and to others.

- They are unable to change unsafe conditions on their own.

Signs of Hoarding[3]
According to the Fairfax County Health Department,
Virginia:[3]

- Extreme collection and storage of items in the home
  and in the yard

- Accumulation of combustible materials (newspapers,
  magazines, and rubbish)

- Blocked exits (doors/windows)

- Narrow pathways in the home

- Rat and/or insect infestations

- Rotting food and/or used food containers

- Human and/or animal waste

- Long-term neglect of home maintenance

- Nonworking utilities, such as heat, running water, sewer, refrigeration

Hoarding is not just a cluttered home or an extensive set of collectibles. Hoarding is the excessive storage of items in and around the home, to the extent that all available space from floor to ceiling may be occupied. People who hoard keep an extreme, disproportionate collection of items, such as newspapers, magazines, empty containers, old clothing, paper, trash, rotting food, and sometimes animals. People who hoard become emotionally attached to everything. They are unable to distinguish trash from treasures. Hoarding "feels right" to people who hoard, in spite of health and safety consequences.

SENIORS

Keep the following in mind when working with senior clients.

Stamina

You may need to schedule shorter sessions (two-hour maximum) because they don't have the stamina physically, emotionally, and mentally to be effective for longer periods of time.

Confusion

Keep things simple for them. Do not create complex systems that will be difficult for them to maintain after you leave.

May be hoarders

Your senior clients may have lived through the Depression and had to live "without" that makes it very difficult for them to let go of unused items.

STUDENTS

Parents need help organizing their children and their homework (typically middle school students with ADD). The challenges of transitioning from one teacher in elementary school to many teachers in middle school often takes students, and parents, by surprise. Many students lack the organizational tools necessary to handle the multiple classes, assignments, projects, teaching methods, and expectations. This all leads to a breakdown in study skills, lower grades, and increased tension between parents and children. What's a parent to do? Don't panic! Consider these simple tips to help your student develop the organizational skills he'll need to succeed in middle school, and in life.

Parents Need to Stay Involved

While middle school is a time of burgeoning independence, parents need to stay involved, at least until their student shows he can manage his own workload. Help your student by creating a routine and habit of the parent checking in with their child each day to review their homework and their projects. Have them check daily to ensure their child has completed his work and packed it in his backpack or binder. When the student returns from school, make sure he's turned it in. For most kids, these daily checks will become habits before long and the parent will be able to relinquish the responsibility.

Make Homework Routine

You can help by making sure the student has a suitable space to work without distractions and with homework supplies nearby. Find a place that's comfortable but not so comfortable he'll fall asleep. Create a routine of setting aside a specific time for doing homework, not just "sometime tonight." Have a really specific time so that gets developed into their routine and becomes a habit also.

Use Tools Wisely

Most middle school students use binders and planners, but many don't use them effectively. Help them to choose a binder with several pockets, then designate the pockets as follows: One for each subject, to hold all completed assignments the teacher has returned; one for all homework to complete, so it's easy to see what needs to be done; and one for homework to turn in, which should be empty at the end of each day. With planners, suggest finding one that shows a week-at-a glance, with blank headings for columns and rows (also known as teacher planner). Designate each column as a day of the week and each row as a subject area or class. Include a row for extracurricular activities as well. This way, students can see everything they have to do on each day. If one day looks heavy and another light (no assignments in one class or no extracurricular activities, for example), help your student determine how to use time on the light day to make the heavier day less hectic. Instruct the student to highlight completed assignments in the planner, and check them off once they're turned in, so you can quickly scan the week for anything not completed and/or turned in.

Teach Time Management

It's the rare middle school student who can gauge how much time an assignment will take. Suggest your student use a timer to develop the skill. If they time themselves reading a fifteen-page chapter, for example, they'll have a good idea how long to allocate when they have to read thirty pages, sixty pages, or more. Plan their week every Sunday night or sometime over the weekend. Instruct the student to write in their planner any known commitments and assignments. Also review what materials might be needed for projects during the week.

Teach Project Management

With longer projects, planners are essential. Suggest students subtract two days from the project's due date for each week they have to work on it. (For a three-week assignment, for example, subtract six days and consider the new date as the due date.) This gives the student a buffer if anything comes up to throw him off schedule. From there, help your student work backward in his planner to create shorter term goals, such as "purchase materials," "complete outline," "finish first draft," etc. This helps them manage their progress along the way and avoid a frantic rush to finish at the end.

Help Them Find Their Own Way

I have learned from my own experience that what works for me and works for my son and works for my husband doesn't work for my daughter. If your method of organization isn't working for your student, help her brainstorm a different method that will work for her.

SAFETY FOR PROFESSIONAL ORGANIZERS

- Dangers you need to be aware may include personal attacks, accidents caused by stacked objects, aggressive animals, or weapons.

- Know your own physical limitations.

- Take an "associate" with you.

- Have your cell phone on.

- If you work alone, refer to your company as "we" instead of "I."

- Use a separate phone number for your business.

- Use a separate post office box address for your business from your home residence address.

- Always let someone know where you are.

- Trust your instincts. If a situation feels uncomfortable, leave immediately.

- It's okay to say 'no'!

---

[1] *Tools for Working with CD & AD/HD Clients,* NSGCD Publication No. 012 2003.

[2] *Conquering Chronic Disorganization,* Judith Kohlberg.

[3] Typical characteristics and signs of hoarding. Fairfax County Virginia www.fairfaxcounty.gov/dpwes/trash/hoarding/typ_character.htm.

In Summary

Organizing as a career can be very rewarding and exciting. It requires the best of your creativity and entrepreneurial spirit. The more successful you want to be and the more dedicated you are to accomplishing your goals, the more you will find and work with your ideal clients–providing you with rich experiences.

I am often asked, "Why do you want to work with people and their messes?" I don't think of my clients that way. I see my clients as individuals who have their own unique talents and gifts, and who just never learned organizing skills. It's no wonder, organizing skills are not taught in traditional educational settings. I am constantly amazed and inspired by the transformations my clients go through after working with me and learning how to live a better life—through organization.

My ADD client Angela is an exciting transformation example I shared with you in Chapter 18. She was interviewed in *More Magazine* to talk about the best investment she ever made in her life, which was hiring a professional organizer. A great testament to our industry that someone thought and publically stated that this was the best investment they ever made. She also lost 50 pounds, a transformation that is not uncommon to my clients. Once clients let go of their clutter they are ready to let go in other areas of their life.

Another transformation example is my client Patty, who after coaching with me decided to launch her own professional organizer business and attended a Professional Organizer Training Institute™ seminar with me.

There are many client stories like Angela and Patty. They are why I work with people to improve their lives through organization. They make my heart sing and make me feel rich!

As a business owner, you have to be your own motivator. You need to keep records, keep your marketing materials updated, plan the direction of your business, and stay informed and educated in the professional organizer industry. This can be difficult and require a great deal of self-discipline. But, the rewards can far outweigh the hard work and go beyond what you ever imagined possible. Learn from my experiences. It doesn't have to take you two years to get your professional organizing business launched and having a full client load like it did me. *Get Rich Organizing* has all of the know-how and tools to get your business off the ground and you running with it in no time. Don't wait—get started now!

Forms and Tools

Client Process Checklists

INITIAL CLIENT CONTACT INFORMATION

Client Name	
Environment	☐ **Residential** ☐ **Home/Small Business** ☐ **Corporate**
Company Name	
Address	
Address 2	
City/State/Zip	
Directions	
E-Mail	
Telephone—home	
Telephone—work	
Telephone—mobile	
Occupation	
Children/Spouse	
Pets	
Budget	
Best day/time to schedule	

First Session date/time	
Referred by or how they heard about us	

- ☐ What prompted them to call you?
- ☐ Explain your approach and process.
- ☐ Communicate your rates.
- ☐ Follow up.
- ☐ E-mail confirmation of appointment and attach PDF of your Services and Fees Agreement.

<u>Intake Conversation Notes:</u>

_____

_____

_____

_____

_____

_____

_____

_____

_____

_____

_____

_____

_____

_____

_____

_____

_____

_____

_____

_____

_____

_____

_____

_____

_____

_____

ONSITE NEEDS ASSESSMENT/
CONSULTATION PREPARATION CHECKLIST

☐ Enter the appointment in your calendar.

☐ Enter the client information in your contacts database.

☐ Prepare and take with you a client file including:

  ☐ Map (directions) to client

  ☐ Client Needs Assessment Questionnaire

  ☐ Organizing Plan of Action template

  ☐ Letter of Agreement (the letter of agreement along with a confirmation of your initial session can be sent via e-mail prior to your session)

  ☐ Invoice for needs assessment (if charging)

☐ Take your camera and tape measure.

ONSITE NEEDS ASSESSMENT/
CONSULTATION APPOINTMENT CHECKLIST

☐ Ask for permission to take "before" pictures and measure areas to be organized.

☐ Complete Client Needs Assessment Questionnaire.

☐ Complete Organizing Plan of Action.

☐ Have client review and sign Letter of Agreement.

☐ Schedule and enter in calendar appointments to complete organizing project.

☐ Present invoice and collect payment for services (if charging).

☐ Prepare summary of initial consultation—assignments/specific Organizing Plan of Action (at assessment/consultation or following).

☐ Handwritten thank-you note (after assessment/consultation if no further appointment or after completion of project).

ORGANIZING APPOINTMENT CHECKLIST

☐ Bring necessary tools, supplies, and products.

☐ Take "after" pictures.

☐ Present invoice and collect payment for services.

☐ Ask client to complete the Client Satisfaction Survey.

☐ Schedule a thirty-day *follow-up* phone call _____.

☐ Handwritten thank-you note (include before/after pictures).

☐ Update your client success stories and reference documents.

☐ Update your Web site.

RESIDENTIAL NEEDS ASSESSMENT QUESTIONNAIRE

Client Name	

Environmental Questions

1. What specifically is not working for you? (Are you organizing their paper, space, or time?)

2. What is working? (Usually you can find something positive.)

3. What is the function of each space and/or how would you like each space to function? (List each room they want you to work in.)

4. Is there too much stuff or not enough storage? (Or some combination of both)

5. What are you willing to part with? (Ask all family members that will be participating)

6. Which family members will be working with us and is everyone agreeable to go through this process?

7. Do you prefer things to be out in view or put away out of sight?

8. What is your vision for this space?

9. What are your goals for this space?

Emotional Questions

If I could ask you to fill in the remainder of these phrases...what would you say?

1. I can never find _____.

2. I don't know what do with _____.

3. When I try to get organized, I struggle with _____.

4. What irritates me the most is _____.

5. What consumes most of my time is _____.

6. I feel I never get a chance to _____.

7. It feels like all I ever work on is _____.

8. I'm really concerned about _____.

History of Disorganization

1. Have you been disorganized most of your adult life?

2. Does your disorganization affect you every day of your life?

3. Have you tried to get organized before?

Expectations

1. What will organized look and feel like to you?

2. What are your expectations of a professional organizer?

3. Do you plan to work with me hands-on or do you prefer to have me work alone and ask you questions as I need to?

4. What must happen for this to be a successful experience for you?

Home Office Questions

Electronic Information Management

1. What type of computer do you use?

2. How many computers are in the office? Are they networked?

3. What operating system are you using and what version?

4. Are you proficient with the computer and its programs?

5. Which electronic information manager do you use (i.e., Outlook)?

6. Do you use all the features offered in your program, such as categories?

7. Do you know your e-mail program well?

8. Do you use a PDA (personal digital assistant)?

9. How do you keep track of your contacts?

10. Do you have an electronic file system?

Time Management

1. Do you have a system in place for planning and tracking your goals and objectives?

2. Do you use a calendar or planner?

3. When do you procrastinate?

Paper Management

1. Can you describe the types of information that you are dealing with in general?

2. Describe how mail and other items arrive in your home.

3. Do you have an in/out tray?

4. Do you have a filing system in place?

5. Do you use your filing system?

6. Does it take you longer than normal to gather materials?

7. Do others need to locate information or items in your possession?

Miscellaneous Notes

_____

_____

_____

_____

_____

_____

_____

_____

_____

_____

_____

_____

_____

_____

_____

BUSINESS NEEDS ASSESSMENT QUESTIONNAIRE

Client Name	

Environmental Questions

1. What specifically is not working for you? (Are you organizing their paper, space or time?)

2. What is working? (Usually you can find something positive.)

3. What is the function of each space and/or how would you like each space to function? (List each room they want you to work in.)

4. Is there too much stuff or not enough storage? (Or some combination of both)

5. What are you willing to part with?

6. Do you prefer things to be out in view or put away out of sight?

7. What is your vision for this space?

8. What are your goals for this space?

Organization Structure and Their Job

1. Can you please give me a brief overview of your business and perhaps your organizational structure?

2. Describe for me the type of business activities you are involved in (meetings, presentations, etc.).

3. What happens in a typical day?

4. How many people work at this location?

5. How many people work for you?

6. Do you have a dedicated assistant?

7. Does your business involve travel?

8. Do you have more than one office location?

Electronic Information Management

1. What type of computer do you use?

2. How many computers are in the office? Are they networked?

3. What operating system are you using and what version?

4. Are you proficient with the computer and its programs?

5. Which electronic information manager do you use (i.e., Outlook)?

6. Do you use all the features offered in your program, such as categories?

7. Do you know your e-mail program well?

8. Do you use a PDA (personal digital assistant)?

9. How do you keep track of your contacts?

10. Do you have an electronic file system?

Time Management

1. Do you have a system in place for planning and tracking your goals and objectives?

2. Do you use a calendar or planner?

3. Who else schedules your appointments?

4. When do you procrastinate?

5. How much time do you spend on the telephone each day?

Paper Management

1. Can you describe the types of information that you are dealing with in general?

2. Describe how mail and other items arrive on your desk.

3. Do you have an in/out tray?

4. Do you have a filing system in place?

5. Do you use your filing system?

6. Are there central files that need to be accessed by others?

7. Do you handle your filing or does someone else?

8. Does it take you longer than normal to gather materials?

9. Do others need to locate information or items in your possession, such as files?

Emotional Questions

If I could ask you to fill in the remainder of these phrases, what would you say?

1. I can never find _____.

2. I don't know what do with _____.

3. When I try to get organized, I struggle with _____.

4. What irritates me the most is _____.

5. What consumes most of my time is _____.

6. I feel I never get a chance to _____.

7. It feels like all I ever work on is _____.

8. I'm really concerned about _____.

History of Disorganization

1. Have you been disorganized most of your adult life?

2. Does your disorganization affect you every day of your life?

3. Have you tried to get organized before?

Expectations

1. What will organized look and feel like to you?

2. What are your expectations of a professional organizer?

3. Do you plan to work with me hands-on or do you prefer to have me work alone and ask you questions as I need to?

4. What must happen for this to be a successful experience for you?

Miscellaneous Notes

_____

_____

_____

_____

_____

_____

_____

_____

_____

_____

_____

_____

_____

_____

ORGANIZING PLAN OF ACTION

Client's name:
Date:
Budget:
Time line:

Room:

Purposes:

1.

2.

3.

4.

5.

Goals:

1.

2.

3.

4.

5.

Ideas for Space:

1.

2.

3.

| 4. |
| 5. |

Assignments:

| 1. |
| 2. |
| 3. |
| 4. |
| 5. |

What materials are currently on hand?

_____

_____

_____

_____

_____

_____

_____

_____

_____

_____

_____

Recommended Materials Needed to Complete Project			
Item	Purpose	Suggested Source	Estimated Cost

FLOOR PLAN

EXAMPLE ORGANIZING COMPANY SERVICES AND FEES LETTER OF AGREEMENT

The purpose of this Letter of Agreement is to confirm the standard XYZ Organizing Company organizing services and fees.

SERVICES

As a full service organizing consultant, XYZ Organizing Company will provide the following organizing services based on your needs.

Initial Consultation and Needs Assessment

❖ <u>Time</u>: *Minimum time is XX hour.*

The purpose of the initial consultation and needs assessment is to identify and define the client's organizing challenges and goals. Since each person's situation is unique, it is critical to get a clear picture of where you are and where you are headed before taking one step forward. The initial consultation takes approximately one hour and involves completing a Client Needs Assessment Questionnaire. In addition to completing the Client Needs Assessment Questionnaire, XYZ Organizing Company will measure and photograph the space to be organized to assist in the implementation process.

Implementation

❖ <u>Time</u>: Varies based on client needs, goals, and participation in the organizing process.

Follow-Up and Evaluation

❖ <u>Time</u>: XX minutes

Once an organizing system is in place and the client has an opportunity to "test" the system, it is important to *evaluate how the system is working.* Within thirty days of implementation, XYZ Organizing Company will provide a thirty-minute follow-up and evaluation session.

Photographs

- May we print your before and after pictures for reference materials? **Yes/ No**

- May we include your before and after pictures on our Web site? **Yes/ No**

- If yes, may we list your name or do you prefer anonymity? **List/Anonymity**

Exclusions: XYZ Organizing Company Professional Organizing Consultants *do not* provide housecleaning, assembly of furniture, shelving, closet systems, moving of heavy furniture, climbing extension ladders, or any similar type of activities.

FEES

Fee Schedule: XYZ Organizing Company organizing services fees (*excluding materials and tools*) are:

Monday–Friday	9:00 AM–5:00 PM	$XX.XX per hour
Monday–Friday	5:00 PM–8:00 PM	$XX.XX per hour
Saturday–Sunday	9:00 AM–5:00 PM	$XX.XX per hour

1. *Initial Consultation and Needs Assessment* fee is due and payable at the end of the consultation.
2. *Implementation* fee is due and payable at the conclusion of each appointment.
3. *Follow-up* fee is no charge for the first thirty minutes. After thirty minutes, the fee is per the above fee schedule and payable at the conclusion of each appointment.
4. *Travel time*

Cancellation Policy: Any appointments cancelled by client with less than ___hours notice to XYZ Organizing Company will be charged for the full amount of the scheduled appointment time.

Limitation of Liability: Client will review all materials XYZ Organizing Company recommends be disposed of by means of recycling, shredding, donation, resale, or any other means agreed to between Client and XYZ Organizing Company. Client agrees that XYZ Organizing Company and its employees are not responsible for any loss of damage caused by Client's failure to carefully review or inspect any disposed items. Client also agrees that XYZ Organizing Company and its employees are not liable for any loss or damage, including consequential damages, Client sustains as the result of services or advice provided to Client by XYZ Organizing Company, or its employees, under this Agreement, including any loss or damage caused by the negligence or fault of XYZ Organizing Company or its employees.

This letter of agreement constitutes the understanding

of standard XYZ Organizing Company organizing services and fees between the parties; its terms can be modified only by a written amendment to this agreement, signed by both parties.

Signature _____ Date: _____

_____, Client
(print or type name)

Signature_____ Date: _____
Professional Organizer's Name, XYZ Organizing Company

TAX PREPARATION CHECKLIST FOR INDIVIDUALS AND SELF-EMPLOYED

General Information
☐ Number of dependents
☐ Social security numbers for each family member

Financial Reports
☐ From personal finance software programs such as Quicken

Tax Filing
☐ Tax preparation instructions for current tax year

Investment Documents
☐ IRA contributions for the year

Bank Statements

Credit Card Year-End Statement Summary

Income Documents
☐ 1099 forms from self-employment and contract work
☐ Alimony received
☐ Business or farm earnings
☐ Federal, state, and local income tax refunds
☐ Income from partnerships or trusts
☐ Income from pensions and annuities
☐ Income from real estate
☐ Interest from investments, savings accounts, etc.

☐ Prize money won

☐ Unemployment compensation

☐ W-2 forms from employer

Charitable Deductions

☐ Cash and in-kind donations

☐ Mileage driving to and from volunteer activities

☐ Other volunteer expenses

Medical Expenses

☐ Medical and dental expenses (if eligible for a medical deduction)

Miscellaneous Expenses

☐ Alimony paid

☐ Education expenses and student loans

☐ Mortgage interest

☐ Moving costs (if relocation is eligible for a deduction)

☐ Tax return preparation costs

☐ Taxes paid (property, etc.)

☐ Unreimbursed employment expenses (travel, lodging, etc.)

Child Care Expenses (if applicable)

☐ Adoption expenses

☐ Child care expenses

☐ Child care provider's tax ID and social security number

Business Expenses (if applicable)

- ☐ Advertising
- ☐ Bank charges
- ☐ Car and truck expenses
- ☐ Commission and fees
- ☐ Depreciation
- ☐ Dues and subscriptions
- ☐ Education or seminars related to business
- ☐ Insurance (excluding health)
- ☐ Interest on business real property
- ☐ Legal and professional services
- ☐ Meals and entertainment (50 percent)
- ☐ Office expenses
- ☐ Outside hiring costs
- ☐ Rent or lease of equipment
- ☐ Repairs and maintenance
- ☐ Supplies
- ☐ Taxes and licenses
- ☐ Telephone, Internet service, cell phones
- ☐ Travel
- ☐ Utilities

TIME MAP / WEEKLY PLAN

Time	Monday	Tuesday	Wednesday	Thursday	Friday	Saturday	Sunday

Time Map

Weekly Plan

ROLE							
Goal							
Goal							
Goal							
Goal							
Goal							
Goal							
Goal							
ROLE							
Task							
Task							
Task							
Task							
Task							
Task							

Weekly Plan

	Monday	Tuesday	Wednesday	Thursday	Friday	Saturday	Sunday
7:00 AM							
7:30 AM							
8:00 AM							
8:30 AM							
9:00 AM							
9:30 AM							
10:00 AM							
10:30 AM							
11:00 AM							
11:30 AM							
12:00 PM							
12:30 PM							
1:00 PM							
1:30 PM							
2:00 PM							
2:30 PM							
3:00 PM							
3:30 PM							
4:00 PM							
4:30 PM							
5:00 PM							

Resources

INDUSTRY ASSOCIATIONS

1. National Association of Professional Organizers (NAPO) www.napo.net
2. Board of Certified Professional Organizers (BCPO) www.certifiedprofessionalorganizers.org
3. National Study Group on Chronic Disorganization (NSGCD) www.nsgcd.org
   - Are You Chronically Disorganized Questionnaire
   - www.nsgcd.org/resources/factsheets/fs001.pdf
   - Common Characteristics of the Chronically Disorganized
   - www.nsgcd.org/resources/factsheets/fs003.pdf
   - Causes of Chronic Disorganization
   - www.nsgcd.org/resources/factsheets/fs004.pdf
   - Tips for Communicating with the Chronically Disorganized
     www.nsgcd.org/resources/factsheets/fs007.pdf
4. Professional Organizers in Canada (POC) www.organizersincanada.com
5. Professional Organizers in Australia, New Zealand, and Hong Kong Australasian Association of Professional Organizers, Inc. (AAPO) www.aapo.org.au
6. Nederlandse Beroepsvereniging van Professional Organizers The Netherlands www.npbo.nl

7. Association of Professional Declutters & Organisers UK (APDO) www.apdo-uk.co.uk
8. National Association of Senior Move Managers (NASMM) www.nasmm.org
9. National Attention Deficit Disorder Association (ADDA) www.add.org
10. People who hoard:
    - NSGCD Clutter Hoarding scale ww.nsgcd.org/resources/clutterhoardingscale.php
    - Fairfax County Virginia www.fairfaxcounty.gov/dpwes/trash/hoarding
    - Children of Compulsive Hoarders www.childrenofhoarders.com

MY TOP TWENTY-FIVE ORGANIZING PRODUCT VENDORS

1. www.archivalsuppliers.com (archival storage)
2. www.busybodybooks.com (calendars, planners, and more)
3. www.containerstore.com (various organizing products, closets, shelving)
4. www.cozi.com (family calendar)
5. www.freedomfiler (filing system)
6. www.homeorg.com (storage systems)
7. www.ikea.com (inexpensive organizing products /furniture/ housewares)
8. www.levenger.com (paper organization)
9. www.livingcookbook.com (recipes)
10. www.momagenda.com (planners, wall calendars)
11. www.myblis.com (a web-based home & life information management system)

12. www.neatnix.com (various organizing products)
13. www.neatco.com (scanner)
14. www.officemax.com (office products)
15. www.organizedatoz.com (various organizing products)
16. www.rev-a-shelf.com (shelving organization)
17. www.russelandhazel.com (office products)
18. www.schoolfolio.com (kids artwork/schoolwork)
19. www.seejanework.com (fun paper and organizing products)
20. www.snapfish.com (photo organization)
21. www.stacksandstacks.com (various organizing products)
22. www.storables.com (various organizing products, closets, shelving)
23. www.tieofficemates.com (kids artwork/schoolwork)
24. www.ultoffice.com (office and paper organizing products)
25. www.westelm.com (decorative and stylish organizing products)

PERIODICALS AND BOOKS
(NOT FOUND ON BCPO LIST PART I CHAPTER 1)

Author	Title
Jeffrey Freed and Joan Shapiro	*4 Weeks to an Organized Life with AD/HD*
David E. Tolin, Randy O. Frost, Gail Sheketee	*Buried in Treasures*
Brian Tracy	*Eat That Frog!*

Author	Title
Laura Leist	*Eliminate Chaos*
Sally Allen	*Independent Contractor Guidebook*
Sari Solden	*Journeys through ADDulthood*
Susan Pinsky	*Organizing Solutions for People with ADD*
Seth Godin	*Purple Cow*
Julie Morgenstern	*When Organizing Isn't Enough SHED*

SPACE PLANNING TOOLS

1. www.morrisathome.com/current/design.aspx
2. www.bassettfurniture.com/tools/room-planner.asp
3. www.ikea.com/ms/en_US/rooms_ideas/splashplanners.html
4. www.boyles.com/room-planner/home-furniture-layout.cfm

WEB SITE DEVELOPMENT

1. www.godaddy.com (create yourself)
2. www.professionalorganizertraininginstitute (Web site development and maintenance)

Logo Design

1. www.thelogocompany.net
2. www.elogocontest.com
3. www.prstore.com

Marketing

1. www.veronikanoize.com (SOHO marketing guru)
2. www.prstore.com

About the Author

Anne Blumer is the owner and founder of SolutionsForYou, Inc., a Portland, Oregon, based company, offering professional organizing services to corporate, home-based business, residential, and small-business clients and offering training programs for professional organizers. Through the Professional Organizer Training Institute™, a division of SolutionsForYou, Inc., Anne has trained hundreds of new professional organizers how to launch, manage, and grow profitable businesses. Anne has extensive experience developing training materials and training professionals in the areas of small-business administration and management, employee benefits, information systems, and mergers and acquisitions. Her experience as a business owner and founder of SolutionsForYou, Inc. Organizing Services has given her skills, knowledge, and the ability to provide complete and *comprehensive* training for individuals.

Anne is among the inaugural 200 professional organizers in the world to receive the Certified Professional Organizer CPO® Designation from the Board of Certified Professional Organizers (BCPO). Additionally, Anne holds a certificate of training from the Coach Approach for Organizers™ and from the NSGCD a Level II ADD Specialist Certificate, Level II Chronic Disorganization Specialist Certificate, Certificate of Study in Learning Styles and Modalities, Certificate of Study in

Chronic Disorganization, Certificate of Study in Basic ADD Issues with the CD Client, and Certificate of Study in CD Client Administration.

After thirteen years as a work-life benefits manager for a high-technology company and seventeen additional years of administrative and managerial positions, Anne launched her career in the professional organizer field.

I became a professional organizer because I discovered that what I loved about all the jobs I previously held was organizing my work environment, projects, and tasks. I also loved helping and teaching my fellow co-workers how to organize their workspace, tasks, and schedule. I feel very fortunate to say I love what I do!

With her years of managerial experience, she understands the organizational skills needed to be a professional in today's competitive business place. As a mother of two children, she also knows firsthand what it takes to organize a busy family and keep a household running smoothly. With this understanding, Anne teaches her clients how to achieve work-life balance through organization, habits, and routines.

Anne is a Golden Circle member of the National Association of Professional Organizers (NAPO), the Oregon chapter of NAPO, and the National Study Group on Chronic Disorganization (NSGCD). As a leader in the professional organizing industry, Anne has served on the NAPO Oregon Board 2003-2009 and is a past president. Anne is the recipient of NAPO Oregon's 2009 President's Award. Anne is NAPO's Education Executive Committee Quality Assurance Director. She has a bachelor's degree in Organizational Communication from Marylhurst University in Oregon. Anne enjoys speaking to a variety of audiences on the benefits of organizing. She has been an active volunteer in her children's schools, passionately teaching students organizational skills.